"Harry Kraemer's *Your 168* goes to the heart of what helps people manage not only their time, but also their energy. All of us can be energized by multiple sources—family, exercise, spiritual well-being. These sources, combined with meaningful work, can lead to a full and integrated life. For anyone who seeks to lead a values-based life, *Your 168* is a personal and inspiring guide to making the most of what matters."

—Alan Mulally
Retired CEO of Ford Motor Company and Boeing
Commercial Airplanes

"I *love* Harry Kraemer's work! He is my role model for exactly what he teaches – *Finding Purpose and Satisfaction in a Values-Based Life*. *Your 168* will help you keep focused on what really matters in life. I could not recommend a better book to help you have a great life!"

—Marshall Goldsmith, two-time *Thinkers 50 #1 Leadership Thinker in the World*, the #1 Executive Coach for 10 years, and
New York Times #1 bestselling author of *Triggers, MOJO,* and
What Got You Here Won't Get You There

"Harry Kraemer elegantly connects his rich legacy of leadership experience with a sense of deep human caring for you in one loving package, capturing the essence of living life with more purpose, meaning, engagement, satisfaction, and fun. After reading this book, I'd be surprised if you're surprised that 168 becomes your favorite number, too."

—Mark C. Thompson, Global Leading Coaches #1 CEO Coach and
New York Times bestselling author of *Success Built To Last: Creating a Life That Matters*

"In *Your 168*, Harry Kraemer helps us to stop and think: What is most important now? How should I use my time? Too often we act before we think, thinking we'll get more done. This book will help you to be mindful, to use your time both more shrewdly and more productively, and in the end to live a life of greater joy and freedom."

—Rev. Francis J. Hoffman, Executive Director/CEO, Relevant Radio

"In *Your 168,* Harry Kraemer offers a wonderful guide for anyone trying to navigate the challenges of a busy life while maintaining meaningful relationships and a sense of self—whether they're leading a multinational organization or just starting out in their career. By encouraging us to reflect on how we spend the 168 hours in our week, Harry gives us the tools to work more productively toward our goals, while staying connected to our personal purpose and values."

—Kelly Grier, U.S. Chair and Managing Partner and Americas
Managing Partner, EY

"Harry Kraemer shows us how to find true personal success based on the pursuit of a balanced life. Funny stories add a lot of humor but do not hide the depth of the message. You will laugh while reading this book—and then you will start reorganizing your life."

—Dr. Francesca Cornelli
Dean, Northwestern University's Kellogg School of Management

"Harry Kraemer's advice about the pursuit of life balance is a great reminder of the importance of acknowledging all that defines us. With greater awareness of *Your 168* and where you devote your time, energy, and ambition, anything is possible! This is a must-read book for a successful and satisfying life."

—Mary Dillon
CEO, Ulta Beauty, Inc.

"Harry Kraemer's *Your 168* is the antidote to any life that feels out of control or lacking in purpose. It offers a treasure chest of insights packed in a plethora of personal examples that will have you nodding, laughing, and learning all at the same time. A retreat in a book—*Your 168* will help you to better know your "true" self and live the fuller, more satisfying life that you deserve!"

—Dr. Bob Nelson
multi-million-copy bestselling author of *1,001 Ways to Reward Employees*

"Harry Kraemer is a visionary leader, mentor, and teacher with a proven ability to drive success at world-class organizations known for never wavering from their core values as they also achieve remarkable results. *Your 168* could be his most important work yet. It's a valuable reminder and guide for each of us that our ability to lead lives with purpose, meaning, and impact starts with the choices we make in how we spend our time."

—Greg Case
CEO, Aon

"In his brilliant new book, Harry Kraemer shows us how to pursue a values-based life with meaning and purpose. Harry's wisdom shines through every story and offers deep insights about living a life with purpose that makes a difference and leaves a legacy for others."

—Bill George, Professor, Harvard Business School; former chair and CEO, Medtronic; and bestselling author, *True North* and *Seven Lessons for Leading in a Crisis*

YOUR 168

FINDING PURPOSE AND SATISFACTION IN A **VALUES-BASED LIFE**

HARRY M. JANSEN KRAEMER JR.

WILEY

Published by John Wiley & Sons, Inc., Hoboken, New Jersey.
Published simultaneously in Canada.

For general information on our other products and services or for technical support, please contact our Customer Care Department within the United States at (800) 762-2974, outside the United States at (317) 572-3993 or fax (317) 572-4002.

Wiley publishes in a variety of print and electronic formats and by print-on-demand. Some material included with standard print versions of this book may not be included in e-books or in print-on-demand. If this book refers to media such as a CD or DVD that is not included in the version you purchased, you may download this material at http://booksupport.wiley.com. For more information about Wiley products, visit www.wiley.com.

Library of Congress Cataloging-in-Publication Data:

Names: Kraemer, Harry M. Jansen, 1955- author.
Title: Your 168 : finding purpose and satisfaction in a values-based life / Harry M. Jansen Kraemer Jr. Other titles: Your one hundred sixty-eight
Description: Hoboken, New Jersey : Wiley, 2020. | Includes index.
Identifiers: LCCN 2020000442 (print) | LCCN 2020000443 (ebook) | ISBN 9781119658542 (cloth) | ISBN 9781119658726 (adobe pdf) | ISBN 9781119658764 (epub)
Subjects: LCSH: Values. | Time management. | Self-realization.
Classification: LCC BF778 .K73 2020 (print) | LCC BF778 (ebook) | DDC 170/.44—dc23
LC record available at https://lccn.loc.gov/2020000442
LC ebook record available at https://lccn.loc.gov/2020000443

Cover Design: Wiley

Printed in the United States of America

10 9 8 7 6 5 4 3 2 1

To everyone—especially my family, friends, colleagues, and students—on the exciting journey of pursuing a values-based life

CONTENTS

ACKNOWLEDGMENTS

Having written about how to become a values-based leader in my first book, *From Values to Action*, and how to build a values-based organization in my second book, *Becoming the Best*, I thought I had addressed most of the major topics discussed in my leadership classes at Northwestern University's Kellogg School of Management. However, my Kellogg students and people who have heard me speak about leadership around the world made it clear that one important pillar was missing from my writing: how does one live a values-based life? So began the journey to *Your 168: Finding Purpose and Satisfaction in a Values-Based Life.*

An amazing number of people have influenced my journey to living a values-based life.

My late parents, Harry and Patricia Kraemer, provided me with a solid foundation and understanding of what it means to live a values-based life, which they passed down from my grandparents, Harry and Elizabeth Kraemer and Farrell and Emily Grehan.

Meeting Julie Jansen at Lawrence University 44 years ago was a defining moment in my life and also affirmed my faith and spiritual direction to live a values-based life. Our 40-year marriage and our five children—Suzie, Andrew, Shannon, Diane, and Daniel—are a constant reminder of the crucial importance of family.

My four siblings—Steve, Paul, Marilyn, and Tom—always remind me that we should not focus on work-life balance but life balance.

I am deeply indebted to my students in the full-time, part-time, and executive MBA programs at Northwestern University's Kellogg School of Management. They are a continual source of reflection and challenge for what it means to pursue a values-based life.

I would also like to thank the following people for sharing their wisdom and personal experiences regarding pursuing a values-based life: Khalid Ali, global marketing director, Dow Chemical; Rob Apatoff, executive director, Kellogg School of Management; Anna Budnik, managing director, Willis Towers Watson; Carter Cast, clinical professor, Northwestern University Kellogg School of Management; J. P. Gallagher, president and CEO, NorthShore University HealthSystem; Fred Harburg, founding partner, AJIL Analytics; Karen May, retired EVP, Mondelez; Dr. Daven Morrison, founding partner, AJIL Analytics; Kevin Murnane, clinical professor, Kellogg School of Management; Jeffrey Solomon, chairman and CEO, Cowen Inc.; Kent Thiry, chairman, DaVita; and Mike Zafirovski, CEO, Zaf Group.

I would like to thank the great work of my publisher, Wiley, especially Jeanenne Ray, Georgette Beatty, and Susan Geraghty, and Andrew Furgal of ImagePros Inc. for the graphics.

Also, a big thank-you to my colleagues, students, and friends who took the time and gave me excellent suggestions and feedback on early drafts of the book, including Khalid Ali, Dan Braga, Jamie McLaughlin, and Ben Zastawny.

Finally, and most important, a very special thanks to Tricia Crisafulli, who has been my trusted collaborator and colleague on all three of my books. For this book, I was also fortunate to work with her son, Patrick Commins, as a key contributor. Without them, this book would not have been possible. Thank you, Tricia and Pat!

—Harry M. Jansen Kraemer Jr.
Wilmette, Illinois

ABOUT THE AUTHOR

Harry M. Jansen Kraemer Jr. is a professor of management and strategy at Northwestern University's Kellogg School of Management, where he teaches in the MBA and the Executive MBA programs. He is an executive partner with Madison Dearborn Partners, one of the largest private equity firms in the United States, where he consults with CEOs and senior executives, and he serves on several for-profit and nonprofit boards. Kraemer is the former chairman and chief executive officer of Baxter International Inc., a multibillion-dollar global health care company. He has been voted Kellogg Professor of the Year in both the full-time MBA and executive MBA programs, including on the Miami and Hong Kong campuses.

INTRODUCTION: THE MOST
IMPORTANT NUMBER

Most of us have at least a general idea of what we think our lives should look like: the kind of work we do, the quality of our personal relationships, our health and self-care, what we do for fun, what role faith and spirituality play in our lives, and the impact we want to make on our community or even on a global scale. We may want all these things, some of these things, or only a few. It's not about following a formula or a prescription—rather it's about *your values* being expressed in the way *you live*.

The challenge, however, is that certain aspects or components of our lives can overshadow the rest. In some cases, they consume so much of our time, energy, and attention that there is not much time left for the other areas we say are important to us. Maybe our work takes almost all our time because we have convinced ourselves that we should be in constant motion. Maybe we focus so much on a leisure activity or sport that it eats away at the time we say we want to spend with other people—family, friends, and loved ones. Or maybe we don't make our health enough of a priority in terms of time commitment. In other words, there's cognitive dissonance: we say certain things are important to us, but our actions don't match those words. There is a disconnect, and not just for a few days or over the course of a busy week or two. I'm talking about chronic imbalance—that feeling of being constantly short of time and attention, always rushing to get things done, and ending each day exhausted and overwhelmed.

1

Without question, we're very active, but are we being productive? Or are we moving so fast, we don't even know? And if we don't know, do we just keep moving because we've confused activity and productivity? As the pace of the world accelerates, and technology blurs the lines between work and home, balance can become an elusive goal. Some people think it's impossible. We start out with good intentions but find ourselves sidetracked, distracted, and even out of control.

To be clear, when I talk about balance, I don't mean work-life balance. If we think about it, that's a confusing concept. The way it is expressed—work-life—seems to indicate a choice that either you're working or you're living. For those of us who work a lot, let's hope work is part of living (if not, we've got a real problem!). We are not just switching from professional to personal, like flipping a switch.

Our lives are multifaceted. We are involved in our careers, but there's more to our lives than just work. We want our lives to have meaning, to lead what I call a *values-based life* in which what we do reflects who we are and what matters most to us. For many of us, that includes spending meaningful time with family, friends, and others in our community. We have outside interests and leisure activities that are important to us and help us feel more balanced. Maybe faith or spirituality is important—even at the center of our lives. Most people want to be healthy and pursue some kind of exercise. Just about everyone I talk to would like to get a little more sleep. And if we think about it, we know we're here in this life for a short period of time and would like to make a difference in our community—and maybe in the world.

These components aren't just lofty goals that sound good or items on a wish list. They reflect our values. By devoting meaningful time to their pursuit, we can lead a values-based life that enables us to be true to ourselves and what we say is most important.

Given how busy everyone is, this doesn't happen by accident. The only way to lead a values-based life is by becoming more self-aware of how and where we spend our time. And that's where *your 168* comes in.

MY FAVORITE NUMBER

Like most math majors, I have a favorite number. Mine is 168. Often, when I ask my students to guess its significance, about one in ten figures it out. It's the number of hours in a week. No matter who you are, what you do for a living, where you live, or how productive you are, you only get 168 hours a week. The only difference is how you spend that time.

It's not about working x hours a week and then having the remaining hours for "other things." It's not working or living, remember? To have true balance among different components of your life—the areas you say are the most important—you need to allocate your time just as you would any precious resource. You accomplish this by being self-reflective and accountable for how you spend your time.

Some people ask me why I don't use 24 hours to divide up a "typical day." For most people (myself included), there is no such thing as a typical day. In my case, on any given day, I may be teaching at Northwestern University's Kellogg School of Management (my graduate school alma mater), traveling across the country to give a speech, working for Madison Dearborn Partners and our private equity portfolio companies, or attending not-for-profit board meetings. Or I could be involved in church activities, spending time with my family, or traveling for leisure. There's no "typical" day.

Over the course of a week, though, our days tend to fall into a pattern. And even if a week is an anomaly—for example, five straight days of business travel—over a few weeks we can see how our time allocation is shaping up. A tool that helps is the life grid, composed of components or what I call *life buckets,* those areas into which you pour your time, attention, and energy.

Table I.1 provides a representation of where and how I want to spend my time and enables me to record how I actually spend my 168 hours a week.

Your life grid may not look like someone else's. And it's not what you think your 168 *should* look like. This is *your* 168—allocated to reflect your priorities, choices, and life circumstances. Being honest and accountable to yourself is fundamental to living a values-based life—otherwise, you're just deceiving yourself, and where's the benefit in that?

Once you have a life grid of how you want to allocate your time, you can start tracking how closely your life follows that plan (see chapter 2). Not every week will be on target. But over time, the goal is to balance your life by keeping track of how you spend your time and holding yourself accountable for your 168.

When I discuss 168 with people, I tend to get two reactions. First, there are those who engage with the idea. They embrace the concept of life buckets to see where they're above or below their goals. They know that no two weeks will be the same. They're

Table I.1   *One example of a life grid with targeted time allocations for each bucket.*

Life Bucket	Goal Hours	Actual Hours Spent	Difference
Career	50 hours (30%)		
Family	28 hours (17%)		
Faith/Spirituality	11 hours (7%)		
Health/Sleep	55 hours (32%)		
Fun/Recreation/ Reading	14 hours (8%)		
Making a Difference	10 hours (6%)		
	168 hours (100%)		

traveling on business one week, so they don't have as much time with family. However, while traveling, they catch up on reading or put in extra hours on a work project, so that when they're back home they can devote more time to family, friends, leisure, and exercise. It's not about beating themselves up; it's about striving to maintain an average over time.

The second reaction from people who hear me discuss 168 is to say, "Wow, that's amazing." (I'm always amused by this reaction because there's nothing that amazing about multiplying 24 hours in a day by 7 days in a week.) What they really mean, I suspect, is that they have no clue as to how they spend their time. They probably haven't taken the time to identify their values and priorities, either. This isn't meant to judge anyone; it's just a fact that not everyone operates with the same level of self-awareness. I can tell you, based on the talks I've given on values-based leadership for the past 15 years, there is a great hunger among people to get their lives back in control with a sense of balance.

That's the goal of *Your 168: Finding Purpose and Satisfaction in a Values-Based Life.* For everyone who wants to live a life with more purpose, meaning, engagement, satisfaction, and fun, 168 should be your favorite number, too.

THE VALUES-BASED LEADERSHIP JOURNEY

For the past 15 years, I have been teaching, writing, and speaking about values-based leadership. In my first book, *From Values to Action: The Four Principles of Values-Based Leadership,* I addressed how anyone at any level can become a values-based leader by following four foundational principles:

- **Self-reflection** to identify and reflect on what you stand for, what your values are, and what matters most
- **Balance** to see situations from multiple perspectives, including differing viewpoints, to gain a holistic understanding

- **True self-confidence** to accept yourself and recognize your strengths and weaknesses, while focusing on continuous improvement
- **Genuine humility** to never forget who you are, appreciating the unique value of each person and treating everyone with respect

From becoming a values-based leader, the next step was to develop a values-based organization, which was the subject of my second book, *Becoming the Best: Build a World-Class Organization through Values-Based Leadership.* This book explored the "five bests" starting with becoming your best self. From there, it's about forming the best team within the organization, being the best partner with customers and suppliers, being recognized as a best investment, and committing to social responsibility as a best citizen.

With the publication of these two books, I have traveled the world delivering more than 1,000 talks (and counting) to several hundred thousand people. The message of values-based leadership resonates as much in the US as it does in Europe, Latin America, and Asia. It applies equally to people in all fields: technology, health care, financial services, retail, academics, and philanthropy. For people at every level—from the CEO to people starting out in their careers and those who are still in school—being a values-based leader in a values-based organization will enhance their lives.

There are challenges. In fact, with every talk I give, people tell me, "This sounds great, Harry, but I'm not sure how I can get all this done. I have so many things going on. How can I do this?"

My answer is this latest book: *Your 168: Finding Purpose and Satisfaction in a Values-Based Life.*

This book is divided into two parts. The first is "Defining Balance." This part begins with the foundation of every values-based leadership discussion: self-reflection. When people tell me that they are having trouble balancing their lives, it's usually because they aren't being self-reflective enough to determine what they are trying to balance. You can only gain clarity on personal and professional issues in your life by thinking more deeply about them. The more self-reflective you are, the easier it is to make choices that are aligned with your values.

Over time, as you become more self-reflective, there are fewer reasons for you to be surprised, which is the next topic of discussion. When people have no idea where and how they spend their time, they're often surprised—and not in a good way. They're suddenly surprised when a relationship fails, friendships end, or loved ones die, leaving them with regret over the time they didn't spend together. At the same time, I know many people who have made meaningful changes in the quality of their lives simply by becoming more aware and eliminating those surprises.

When surprises go unheeded, they don't just fade away. Without the self-awareness that comes from self-reflection, a relatively minor surprise or small problem compounds into a major upset—and you hit the brick wall. Now you've got a full-blown crisis on your hands. As I've seen among people I know, including those who have shared their life journeys with me, these crises often spill over into numerous areas: a major relationship is in turmoil, someone's health suffers, a job is in jeopardy. When you hit a brick wall, it can cause wreckage everywhere in your life.

Next, we'll talk about building new habits, which takes both awareness and time. Research tells us that it takes three months on average to build muscle memory (such as engaging in a new exercise routine) and even longer to adopt new health habits or ways of thinking and acting.

The discussion then moves to becoming more planful and constantly reprioritizing. Life doesn't stand still. Priorities and demands change. The only thing that remains constant is 168!

Reprioritizing requires you to consider how demands on your time are changing and whether these new demands fit your values. The reward for being more planful is increased flexibility and greater spontaneity. All that discipline in planning and reprioritizing pays off when suddenly there's a surprise opportunity—like two tickets to see your favorite musician in concert—and you can make the time for fun.

The second part is "The Balancing Action Plan." In this part, we move from what defines a balanced life to putting an action plan in place to create greater balance. We explore six life buckets and how people at all phases and stages devote time and energy to each of these buckets:

- **Work and career** (with the pursuit of balance in real time). For most of us, work is very important and must get done. However, today more than ever, it's possible to use technology and flexible arrangements to make working part of your life. In this chapter, we'll also discuss how to tackle two buckets at once—not as a rule, but strategically. This is all about investing your 168 in ways that work for you.
- **Family, friends, and community.** Our lives are enriched by the people who matter most to us. For many, this means family and friends, but it can also include support groups and community organizations. By choosing whom we spend time with, when, and for how long, we can build meaningful and supportive communities for ourselves.
- **Health.** One of the most common desires I hear is to "be healthier"—and one of the common complaints is "I don't have time for it." But we know that health directly affects quality of life, which means health goals for most people are a priority in their 168.
- **Fun.** Life needs fun. Too often, though, fun seems like the last priority for people, and without planning for fun, it can get overlooked.

- **Faith and spirituality.** For many people, having a life bucket for faith and spirituality is critically important. It reinforces self-reflection and embraces one's purpose at a deeper level.
- **Making a difference.** Many of us want to make a positive impact—big or small. For some, it's in the local community; for others, it's global. In your own way, you can allocate your 168 in a way that creates a legacy.

No one's life is in balance all the time. We are all works in progress, constantly refining ourselves through self-reflection and becoming more self-aware. As we become more aware of our values and of how we spend our time, however, we move closer to the goal of leading a values-based life.

We're each given 168 hours a week. It's up to us to spend them in a way that matters most.

DEFINING BALANCE

CHAPTER 1

BECOMING
SELF-AWARE

To live a values-based life, you need to know what your values are. Then, you make a sincere and ongoing effort to live your life so that what you do and how you act reflect those values. Sounds pretty straightforward, doesn't it? But notice I said, "sincere and ongoing effort." The reality is no matter how dedicated you are to living a values-based life, you're always a work in progress. Nobody gets it right all the time. In my more than 40 years of pursuing a values-based life, I'm constantly recalibrating how to allocate my 168 hours each week to reflect my values and what I believe is most important in my life. That's the only way I know of to pursue life balance.

Life balance, as I explained in the introduction, doesn't mean work-life balance—a concept that always confused me because it seems to indicate a choice between working and living. Our lives are multifaceted. Many of us devote a great deal of time to work—let's hope, doing work we find meaningful and satisfying. But there is more to our lives than work. We have other priorities that might include family, friends, and/or others within our community. We have leisure activities that bring enjoyment and enrich our lives. We want to be healthy and pursue some kind of exercise. Spirituality may be important, and maybe we want to make a positive impact in the community or even globally.

Don't mistake life balance for time management. The primary goal here is not to become incredibly efficient with your time, although that might be one of the benefits of engaging in this process. The primary goal is life balance. It comes down to the life buckets I discussed in the introduction, the specific areas into which we allocate our time, attention, and effort. By focusing on our chosen life buckets, we can pursue life balance—with the caveat that we won't be in balance all the time. Rather, we'll be constantly recalibrating and rebalancing.

The only way to pursue life balance is by becoming self-aware through self-reflection. Your commitment to living your life aligned with your values won't always be easy. Countless demands, distractions, and unexpected challenges will get in the way. But the payoff for engaging in the pursuit of life balance is to have more joy, satisfaction, purpose, and meaning, with a lot less worry, fear, anxiety, pressure, and stress.

THE REALITY CHECK

Whenever I talk about life balance, most people are very intrigued. They ask whether it is really even possible to be self-reflective in the crazy, nonstop world in which we live. I always tell people that a large part of the problem is that most of us are attempting to do three to four times the number of things that is humanly possible. We tell ourselves we'll "make time" as if we can somehow manufacture more hours in the day or week. (Sorry, but there are only 168 hours in the week for everybody.) We want to be conscientious and get as much done as possible, so we tell ourselves we'll just go faster. What other choice is there given all we have to do? So that brings us to our old friend, multitasking. We convince ourselves that if we can do two (or more) things at the same time, we'll get twice as many (or more) things done!

Our smartphones and other devices are supposed to make us more productive. We're connected all the time and everywhere. But it's getting out of control. It's one thing to do a call while you're driving, but quite another to do email and texts at red lights—or when traffic slows to a crawl. You'll soon drive yourself crazy, not to mention potentially become a hazard on the road.

At some point, you have to ask yourself: are you really more productive or just more active? Have you confused activity for productivity? If you're moving so fast, however, you won't have any idea how productive you are—and you'll just keep moving.

That's when you need to take some time, step back, and self-reflect. What are you spending your time on? How does that match with what you say is most important in your life? That's the only way to cut through the activity and get to productivity so you can pursue a balanced life. If you want life balance, you need self-reflection.

EMBRACING SELF-REFLECTION

"Wait a minute, Harry, I don't have time for that!" Be honest: was that your first response? Trust me, after more than 15 years of teaching and giving talks on values-based leadership, I hear this all the time. "Sounds great, but I don't have time for that. I'm traveling half the time, my to-do list is eight miles long, and everybody in my life wants more of me."

When people say that, I cannot help but wonder if it's really an issue of not having the time (we're talking about 15 minutes a day) or if this is just something they don't want to do. If people were really honest with themselves, maybe the reason they don't want to self-reflect is they don't want to confront the truth that there is a very big difference between what they say is important and how they allocate their 168 hours. Being self-reflective can get uncomfortable because it's too close to home. So let's address that first: self-reflection isn't about beating yourself up. It's about being truthful with yourself about what is—and is not—a priority for you. There's no judgment here. Your self-reflection is just for you, to pursue more balance in a way that makes the most sense for your life—not someone else's life.

If you want to lead your own life, and not be in a constant state of reacting to others, it makes sense to take some time for self-reflection. This can take as little as 15 minutes—ideally every day, but even once a week is a good start. I've practiced self-reflection since I was in high school, all the way through college and then graduate school; from the earliest days of my career all the way to becoming chief financial officer and then chief executive officer of Baxter International, a $12 billion health care company with 52,000 employees. Today, I teach at Northwestern University's Kellogg School of Management; I'm an executive partner at Madison Dearborn, a private equity firm; I work closely with companies in our portfolio and sit on several boards; and I travel 60 percent of the time, including to give speeches on values-based leadership to people around the globe. And my wife, Julie, and I have been married for 40 years and have five children; my spiritual life is very important to me; I exercise five days a week; and I stay in touch with family and many close friends. Trust me, I know all about being busy. But I also know that, without self-reflection, there would be no way I could pursue balance in all the things that are important to me and live a life that is an authentic reflection of my values.

So where do you find the time? You have 15 minutes, some-where.

Most of us have to commute by train, bus, or car. You can devote some of that time to self-reflection. If you exercise, you can engage in self-reflection on the stationary bike, elliptical, or treadmill or while you're jogging. If you pray or meditate, you're already beginning the practice of self-reflection. These times can help you reflect on what really matters to you and why.

To be clear, self-reflection is not self-absorption. You're not contemplating the cosmos—or your navel. You're asking yourself some probing questions that give you clarity on how you want to allocate your 168 hours and keep you accountable for how those hours are being invested. When you engage in self-reflection for the first time, you need to establish a baseline for yourself. You need to slow down, turn off the noise, and be by yourself. There are some basic, yet very important, questions to ask yourself, such as these:

- What are my values?
- What do I stand for?
- What is my purpose?
- What really matters?

As a daily practice of self-examination, I tend to self-reflect at the end of each day, after I've completed my work and I've had time with my family. By midnight or so, I've finished my phone calls and emails and I've had time to exercise. In those quiet moments, I take 15 minutes to reflect on my day. Sometimes, I'll take a half hour or longer, depending on what is going on in my life. This dedicated time for self-reflection has become a habit like brushing my teeth. For me, it is the perfect way to end my day and to give myself clarity and a way forward for the day ahead. For example:

- What did I say I was going to do today, in all dimensions of my life?
- What did I actually do today?
- What am I proud of?
- What am I not proud of?
- What would I do differently if I could live today over again?
- Knowing what I know now, how will I act tomorrow?

You may ask similar questions, or they may be very different depending on your priorities, values, and circumstances. Ask yourself questions that are most relevant to you. It may be worthwhile to record your reflections in a journal, especially to review your thoughts later. I find this extremely helpful, because writing down my self-reflection not only increases my self-awareness but also provides a structure that keeps me from slipping into daydreaming. Day after day, my self-reflection journals provide a record of where I am and what I'm thinking at any given time.

The more frequently you self-reflect, the more you'll already know your values, your purpose, and what really matters. This will enable you to spend more time on the questions that keep you accountable to yourself for how you're living your life. But that won't happen if you're trying to do ten things at once. Take some time to think about these questions to put your life into perspective. As you prioritize, you'll separate activity and productivity. What seems infinitely complicated can be broken down into discernable parts to be addressed and dealt with in a reasonable way. Or, as I like to say, I can get from the roots to the trees to the forest!

MY SELF-REFLECTION JOURNEY

Although self-reflection is a major part of my life, it was something I had to learn. I am very fortunate that I had experiences when I was young that introduced me to the kind of thinking about myself and the world that I practice today as self-reflection. I can remember being seven years old and walking around Central Park in New York City with my maternal grandfather, Farrell Grehan. He was a history teacher and would discuss historical figures and important events, all the way back to the times of the ancient Greeks and the Roman Empire.

One day I asked, "Grandpa, why are there always wars?"

He replied, "Harry, since the dawn of humankind, people have killed each other. Part of it is that people don't take the time to listen to one another and don't reflect on how short of a time they're on this earth. Therefore, they're only after power and wealth, things that are very temporary."

My grandfather would look down at me and say, "It was only a blink of an eye ago that I was a child like you." That always seemed incredible to me. I began to grasp what he meant when he said, "We're here for a very short time."

As I got older, I began to think more about the shortness of life and what I could do while I'm here. My father had a great line—he may have even stolen it, but he sure could deliver it: "Have you ever seen a hearse going to a cemetery with a U-Haul attached to it?" He always got a good laugh from that one, but beyond the punchline there was a serious message. Dad would say, "Most people must think they're either going to live forever or they're going to take all of this material stuff with them."

I can remember when I was 13 years old and we were living in northeastern Pennsylvania. I was really into cars and liked to look at the front grilles and figure out their make and model. I'd see a particular grille and know the car was a Ford or an Oldsmobile.

Back in those days, there were big fields filled with junk cars that were sold for parts or scrap metal. One day, Dad and I were driving past a big flatbed truck carrying a huge stack of flattened cars. Dad looked out the window and asked me, "What's the grille on the third one from the bottom?"

"That's a Mercedes," I replied.

Dad shook his head. "You know, about ten years ago, some guy bought that car and was so proud of it. He'd always park it at the very end of the parking lot so no one would put a ding in the door. Didn't matter if it was raining, he'd be the farthest from the door so nothing would happen to his car. And now look, that same car is flat as a pancake on the back of a flatbed truck."

That made quite an impression on me. Dad wasn't against material possessions and neither am I. You work hard, you do well, so you want to have a nice house and car. It's okay to treat yourself. But don't be possessed by your possessions. Self-awareness can help you discern what you need and why you need it—and, of course, what you don't need at all.

Another pivotal moment in my development as a self-reflective person was a conversation I had with my uncle, my dad's brother, who was a priest in northeastern Pennsylvania. Father Francis would come over to the house on Friday evenings (for a fish dinner, naturally), and afterward he would play pinochle with my parents. One night, when I was about 14 or so, I asked to speak with my uncle after dinner.

"There's something I want to tell you—I've been thinking about this a lot." I took a deep breath. "I think I want to become a priest."

My uncle was ecstatic. "Oh, this is great. You have a calling!"

I wasn't nearly as excited as my uncle. "You see, this is where I'm confused: I don't think I really have a calling. But every Sunday we hear that there is a serious need for more priests, and we pray for more people to join the religious orders. The fact is, we need more priests. And knowing my friends, trust me, we'd be in big trouble if one of them becomes a priest. If someone is going to pull the short straw here, it might as well be me."

If my uncle felt disappointed, he didn't show it. Instead, he said to me, "First of all, it's pretty clear to me you don't have a calling. But if you live your life the right way, you can have an enormous impact on others."

My uncle explained that, as a priest, he could affect only those who came to church, and as important as his parish was to him, it was a pretty small group. "But, Harry, if you end up going into business or teaching, you could influence so many more people. Through your example and behavior, you could make a positive impact on more people than you can imagine."

I breathed a huge sigh of relief: "This is great news because I don't want to become a priest." But I did like the idea of making a positive impact, starting with myself—in the choices I made, in the way I treated other people.

Finally, there is another personal component to my self-reflection. In addition to my daily reflection, every year in early December I attend a silent retreat to think deeply about what matters to me. As the Jesuits who run the retreat explain, in silence we are able to "dispose ourselves" so that we can really listen to our inner thoughts. When we are silent and remove ourselves from the conversation, we listen on a deeper level. This retreat provides me with a few precious days free from phones and emails. All gadgets and devices are put away. There are only paper, a pen, and silence to dive into the key questions of who I am, what my values are, and what difference I want to make during the short time I am on this earth. And remember those self-reflection journals I've been keeping for 40 years? Three days of complete silence are the perfect time to review the past year, what I said I would do, how well (or poorly) I've kept these commitments, and where I can improve.

From my days as a youth until today, self-reflection has been an anchor of my life. I took this habit with me when I went off to college at Lawrence University, where I received a degree in mathematics and economics, and then graduate school at Northwestern University's Kellogg School of Management for my MBA in finance and accounting. Self-reflection was a personal habit when I began my career, and in time, it became my foundation as a values-based leader.

Today, I'm privileged to teach values-based leadership at Kellogg and to give speeches and presentations on this topic to people around the world. I'm always touched by how much values-based leadership and leading a values-based life resonate with people. I'm grateful that these interactions are meaningful to others, and they help refresh me as I continue on my own values-based leadership journey. But I also know through several decades of personal experience that living a values-based life is not possible without self-reflection. It is the only way to discover your values, identify your priorities and what matters most, and pursue a balanced life.

WHAT GOES UP ALWAYS COMES DOWN (AND VICE VERSA)

Even my best sales pitch for self-reflection as the key to pursuing life balance doesn't convince everyone. If you are still on the fence, then consider this: self-reflection is the best way I know to minimize worry, fear, anxiety, pressure, and stress. Who wouldn't want that? Not only are these emotions distracting and unproductive, they're also unhealthy.

Once you're worrying about a problem, it's too late: worry has already set in. As you worry, you feel fear and anxiety, and then the pressure and stress start mounting. The solution is not to wait until you're in the middle of a problem or, worse yet, that problem has become a crisis. Rather, you want to increase your awareness and identify all the things that could happen in a given scenario and how you'll respond. Then, no matter what happens, you'll know what to do because you've thought it through in advance.

No one can avoid problems—they are inevitable. It's not a matter of if, but when. You won't know the timing or the details, but you can be assured that at some point you'll face challenges—personal, professional, or both.

Figure 1.1 is an illustration I use in my classes.

I have yet to meet anyone whose life just constantly gets better and better. The reality is we experience ups and downs, a series of high points followed by low points—we hope with an overall upward slope. You can plot the highs that you've already experienced—those events you look back on and say, "That's when life was going really well." And you know those low

No matter what we might want, our lives don't go like this:

Instead our lives look like this:

Figure 1.1   *Your life trajectory will never be a straight line. Rather you will experience many ups and downs along the way.*

points you've gone through, when life was difficult because of disappointments, losses, and setbacks.

As you look to the future, you know there will be more high points and more low points to come. Given that realization, you know that when things are going great, it's only a matter of time when some problem or challenge arises. The only question is how you will react.

With the benefit of more than 40 years of self-reflection, I know that when things are going well, I will be grateful and enjoy the moment. I will thank everyone who helped make it happen. I will find a way to really take in those good times and make them special: have a party to celebrate—even getting little crazy with a case of Chablis and some baby shrimp. However, before the party ends, I will ask myself what I will do when (not if) problems and challenges arise. That's when I know I will do two things: the first thing is, no matter what happens, I'm going to do the right thing. The second is I'm going to do the best I can. There's an enormous assumption here, of course: what is the right thing to do?

To prepare for that inevitability, all of us need people we can rely on who share our values. They are our sounding boards for helping us discern the right thing to do, especially if their perspectives are different than yours. (And, in the same way, you'll be a sounding board for them, too.) How do you find these people? They're among your family, friends, colleagues, and associates.

Let's say you've been working with someone who seems to be a self-reflective person. You make a point to invite this person to lunch and have a conversation about what's most important to him or her. You share a little about your sense of purpose and how you find meaning in what you do.

It takes me about 15 minutes of conversation to figure out whether someone is self-reflective or not. People who think deeply about things, who go beyond what's obvious or who don't view everything as "what's in it for me," really stand out from the rest. These are the people you want to have in your inner circle, who will accompany you on your life journey and help you when you get off track. Even asking someone, "What matters most to you?" will give you insights. It's not only what they say, but how they say it. Do they answer as if they've thought about this before? Or is the concept completely unfamiliar?

Your sounding board isn't just for crisis response. Getting and giving input within a close group of people helps you maintain the balance that, as we all know, can be a moving target. And, to be honest, any of us can fall victim to rationalization. My wife, Julie, has said to me that, left to my own devices, I could convince myself of just about anything. So when she asks me, "Do you want to know what I think?" after 40 years of marriage, I know the only answer is "Yes!" Having close, trusted people as your sounding board will keep you honest with yourself.

It may be a case of having 50 things on your to-do list and believing you can magically create the time to get it all done. A friend/advisor who knows you well can point out the obvious: there is no way you can do all that you say you can do, and you'll only drive yourself crazy (along with everyone around you) as you futilely try.

Or you may be increasingly aware that you're out of balance. There are so many pressures on you and priorities competing for your time and attention (often work-related), and you just can't see a way forward. Guilt, frustration, exhaustion, and a general feeling of being overwhelmed may convince you that balance is impossible. But someone in your circle can give you an outside perspective, often from his or her own life experiences when faced with similar pressures or situations. Just knowing that someone had the same challenges and found a way through them can be greatly encouraging. Moreover, that person can help you find ways in which to experience more balance, to make choices, to give yourself permission to say no to what isn't a priority, and to find a way back to the center.

There may be times, too, when your life gets out of balance and you can't (or won't) see it. You say that something is important (family, health, etc.), but your choices reflect the exact opposite. Someone close to you can give you the reality check you need by pointing out that your words and actions aren't aligned. You're trying to project one image, but your actions display something else—in the most extreme, you've become a Dr. Jekyll and Mr. Hyde story. That kind of feedback can be a wake-up call that gets you back on track quickly, living the kind of life that is true to who you are and what you value.

Research shows just how important these outside perspectives are. Tasha Eurich, an organizational psychologist and researcher, observed that just asking yourself why you did something (or failed to do something) is not sufficient because many people do not have access to their unconscious thoughts, feelings, and motives. To help them discern their behaviors and why they behave the way they do, Eurich writes that people need to seek out "honest feedback from loving critics."[1] With this outside feedback and per- spective, people can see themselves more clearly, which increases self-knowledge along with self-awareness. This kind of feedback, plus regular (ideally, daily) self-reflection by asking yourself probing questions, greatly enhances self-awareness.

RECALIBRATING YOUR LIFE BALANCE

I am often asked by students and executives alike: how do you know if you are really self-reflective and becoming self-aware? At the risk of being morbid, I tell the following story: imagine for a moment that after your annual physical, your doctor wants to meet with you. "I've been going through the results of your tests," the doctor tells you, "and I'm going to be honest with you: you only have three days to live."

Facing your imminent mortality, would you start feeling regret about what you wished you'd done differently? Are there people you've become estranged from? Do you regret broken relationships? Are you consumed with anger and resentment? Do you feel remorse for having taken advantage of someone? Then why not avoid all that now!

All of us are going to have three last days—we just don't know when they're going to be. Self-reflection helps us identify those areas in our lives we need to repair now. We own up to past mistakes, make amends where we can, forgive ourselves and others, and make the most of the time we have. Moving forward, we commit to treating people exactly as we would like to be treated (they don't call it the Golden Rule for nothing). Self-reflection can give you the peace of mind that you are sincerely trying to do the best you can every day, while being accountable to yourself for where and how you can do better.

Your life won't be perfect, but I guarantee it will get better. You will have more gratitude during the good times, because self-reflection will help you pause and be thankful. You'll have more peace of mind and clarity during challenging times, because you're committed to doing the right thing and doing the best you can do. Your worry, fear, anxiety, pressure, and stress will be greatly reduced, although not eliminated—welcome to being human! And there are folks who say a little bit of pressure may be helpful for getting things done. Unfortunately, that "little bit" of pressure can often become a lot and affect your health. But if you hunger for a life with more balance among those things that mean the most to you, self-reflection should become a regular habit.

Self-reflection isn't about perfection. You won't be perfectly balanced every day or even most days. We have busy lives and many things vie for our time and attention. Priorities change and challenges arise.

There is no formula or perfect answer to achieving life balance. It's a constant process of recalibration. Week to week as you look at your 168 hours, you'll see where you are in balance and out of balance. You'll make choices going forward to rebalance—more time with family, doing better with daily exercise, spending time with friends you haven't seen in a while. But our lives are too busy and complex to expect that we'll always be in balance. There will always be things that force us out of balance again.

Self-reflection, I've found, is the best foundation for creating and sustaining life balance. This is not the pursuit of perfection, but of greater self-awareness. When we know where and how we're spending our time, when things are going well or when we feel we're going off the rails, we can find a way forward.

NEXT STEPS TO BETTER BALANCE

In the pursuit of life balance, we're all works in progress. At the end of each chapter, starting here, I'll share some advice and exercises that can help you become more self-aware as you take active steps toward achieving better balance in support of your 168.

First-Time and Annual Self-Reflection Questions

As you engage in self-refection for the first time, ask yourself these questions to begin the process of regular self-examination. In addition, I use these same questions on my annual retreat:

- What are my values?
- What do I stand for?
- What is my purpose?
- What really matters?
- How would I react if I was told I only had three days to live?
- What kind of person do I want to be?
- What kind of example do I want to be for others?

Daily Self-Examination Questions

As you engage in regular self-reflection, ask yourself questions that help you evaluate your day and think about how you spend your time. Here are the questions I use every day:

- What did I say I was going to do today, in all dimensions of my life?
- What did I actually do today?
- What am I proud of?
- What am I not proud of?
- What example did I set for others?
- What example did others set for me?
- If I could live today over again, what would I do differently?
- If I have tomorrow (and I am acutely aware that one day I won't), based on what I learned today, what will I do tomorrow in all dimensions of my life that are important to me?

CHAPTER 2

WHY ARE YOU SURPRISED?

Often when I'm traveling, I run into former students in airports. (There are many of them out there—I've been teaching for 15 years.) I'm always happy to see them and to catch up with what's going on in their lives. Many of these former students have had significant events in their lives since they graduated from Kellogg: getting new jobs, getting promoted, getting married, having children. But every few weeks, the encounter is a little different: for some of these former students, life hasn't turned out the way they expected.

I had one of these encounters while I was at Chicago's O'Hare Airport. A former student appeared tense and nervous, so when I asked him, "How's it going?" I was prepared to hear some bad news.

"To tell you the truth, not so good," he told me. "I'm traveling all the time for my job. I have two young boys now and I have no relationship with them." Then came the kicker: "Harry, I'm so surprised."

I said I was sorry to hear that, then asked how much time he spends with his sons.

"I don't really spend any time with them at all. I'm hardly home."

And I wondered: why is he surprised that he doesn't have a relationship with his sons?

Another incident occurred recently, just before class. I noticed one of my students was clearly upset. When I asked her what was wrong, she told me her grandfather had passed away a few days ago. It was such a shock, she said. She had wanted to spend more time with him, to get his insights on life, but now he was gone. "It happened so suddenly," she told me. "I was so surprised."

I expressed my condolences and then asked how old her grandfather was.

"One hundred and two."

At the risk of sounding insensitive, I have to tell you: when someone who has lived to be more than a century old passes away, that's not "sudden." Given his age, when was she planning to get together with him—in six months? A year? Of course, I didn't say any of those things, but I have to admit that I was tempted to ask, "Why are you surprised?"

Make no mistake, I have compassion for others. Everyone has disappointments, setbacks, and sadness in their lives, and I'm no exception. A relationship breaks up. You don't get the job you wanted, or the promotion you worked so hard for goes to some- body else. Someone you love and care deeply about passes away. All of this is very unfortunate, but it really shouldn't be a surprise—not if you're self-reflective.

BECOMING MORE AWARE

Self-reflection isn't a crystal ball. You won't be able to project every possibility and its outcome. But with regular self-reflection, you'll become more self-aware. You'll become increasingly attuned to every facet of your life, especially those areas that you haven't paid enough attention to. You'll pick up on the cues when your life is out of balance and you're running into trouble. With self-examination, you know when it's been too long since you've checked in with a close friend or family member. You'll keep tabs on your health, sleep habits, spirituality, time for leisure or fun—or whatever your priorities are. That alone will greatly reduce many of those "surprises" because you'll be proactive about making changes to ward off many problems and upsets. And for those you can't avoid, as I outlined in chapter 1, you'll do the right thing and the best you can do.

This all seems so straightforward, and yet some people have a hard time grasping how self-reflection can minimize surprises that have "suddenly" upended their lives. The more I think about it, the more I realize that intelligence seems to be inversely proportional to being able to minimize surprises. As I've observed, some of the brightest, most conscientious, and driven people are often the most prone to falling victim to surprises.

Let me give you an example. I can't tell you how many students come to my office to discuss two job offers they're weighing. Often these job offers are from consulting or investment banking firms. For a young associate joining these firms, it's going to be extremely demanding.

The first thing I ask is why they are pursuing this path. Nearly every time, they don't have a real answer. They haven't spent much time thinking about it. Now these are some of the best students, and yet they have trouble answering the question "Why do you want to take this particular type of job?" With a little probing, it usually boils down to the simple fact that they're following *other* top students who are taking this path. Their thinking is "If they're doing this, then I should, too."

The issue is they're focusing on what someone else is doing. That's a formula for living a life that probably won't be the best for you. Consider the example of another former student I ran into while I was waiting for a flight at New York's LaGuardia Airport. As we caught up with each other, she explained that she was working

90 hours a week, traveling 90 percent of the time, and spending very little time with her fiancé.

When she told me she was surprised that she had no personal time, I thought, "Did you not read the job description before you signed up?" A Google search of *burnout* in management consulting and investment banking will give you an eyeful. Most insightful of all would be to talk with someone whose values and priorities align with yours who is in that field and ask the question "What's your life like?"

Now, for some people, life on the road is exactly what they want. Ram Charan, the famed management consultant, earned a reputation not only for counseling the top CEOs in the world but also for traveling constantly. As a *Fortune* profile of him from several years ago stated, "Charan never stops. He sleeps in a hotel every night . . . except when he's sleeping on a plane or, rarely, in someone's house."[1] But this is Ram's choice—he is wired for this kind of lifestyle and he clearly enjoys it. He realizes what he's choosing and is not surprised.

In the same way, how you spend your 168 must be based on your individual choices. If you decide you're going to take that job with a lot of travel, understand what that really means. Whatever you do, make sure you go into it with your eyes wide open. Whether you become the next road warrior consultant, or you open a tea shop in a small town, give it real thought. You need to be self-reflective: does this job or other life choice support or undermine what matters most to me? Will I be able to pursue a balanced life as I define it? Or am I getting myself into something that will result in me being out of balance most of the time?

You have multiple life buckets, remember? Friends, fun, sports, going to movies—all these leisure activities may be very important to you. So is having time for work and getting ahead in your career. (I get it—I was chairman and CEO of a $12 billion health care company with more than 50,000 employees.) But if you aren't self-reflective, some of your life buckets are going to be overflowing and others will be empty—and you'll be surprised.

THE COST—AND CONSEQUENCE— OF BEING UNAWARE

People who aren't self-reflective are constantly surprised. Something they didn't expect occurs, and they get blindsided. Usually they have no idea what just happened, why it happened, or what to do next. The reason they are constantly surprised is fairly simple: if you aren't aware of how you spend your time, you won't have a grasp of what matters most. If you're unaware, it's easy to convince yourself that "everything is fine" and that you'll have time to take care of things "later." Then a week turns into a month, then six months, then a year. . . During that time, the people you say are most important may not be waiting around for you. They've moved on—sometimes literally. One guy I knew was traveling so much that when he was finally home and his significant other wasn't there, he didn't think much about it. It never occurred to him to wonder why. Then he found out that she had actually left several months earlier—and he never even noticed.

All of us are capable of rationalization. People might be tempted to say, "Hey, 50 percent of relationships don't seem to last anyway. It's unfortunate that my relationship ended, but at least I've got my children." But children aren't blind to the fact that Mom or Dad hasn't been around for the past few years. When a parent who has been mostly absent for the past four or five years suddenly decides it's time for some "quality" time together, it shouldn't be a surprise when the children prefer not to have them around.

I don't say this to embarrass or judge anyone. It's not my place to say how people should live their lives. I won't recommend choices for you or anyone else. Everyone is different! You need to decide what works for you according to your values and what matters most to you.

As you know by now, I believe self-reflection is the best way to determine whether your life is really working for you. You'll see where things are starting to come apart—the relationship that's damaged, the friendship that's strained, the health risks you're trying to ignore, your irritability because you aren't sleeping enough or taking care of yourself. The sooner you notice when things are off, the quicker you can intervene by rebalancing. Remember, no one is in balance all the time—or even most of the time. We're constantly pursuing life balance because the reality is we are very busy people who are often out of balance! We're traveling for business, we're juggling family responsibilities, we're trying to enjoy leisure activities.

If you don't check in with yourself through self-reflection, it's easy to become one-sided. You're down to one or two life buckets, while the other areas of your life are empty. And what happens in those neglected parts of your life? You guessed it—that's where you get "surprised."

COGNITIVE DISSONANCE

Many years ago, a senior executive—let's call him Bill—came to see me on a Friday afternoon to ask for some advice. Things weren't going well for him, Bill told me. He was having problems with his spouse and his three children. "Harry, you're married, and you've got five kids. I thought you could share some perspective with me."

I told him I'd be happy to sit down and listen. Although I never think of myself as having the answers, I do have opinions. "How about getting together on Saturday?"

"Can't," Bill told me. "I'm golfing all day Saturday."

"No problem. How about Sunday? You can come over any time after church."

"Yeah, I'm actually golfing on Sunday, too."

Now, I have nothing against golf, but I do know that it takes about five hours to play 18 holes. Two days of golf equals 10 hours. Maybe golf was very important to Bill. Maybe he was a fabulous golfer, and this was a real passion for him. If so, spending a good portion of the weekend golfing might make sense for him. However, the problem, from what I could tell, was Bill said family time was a big priority, but his actions conflicted with his words.

That's what psychologists call *cognitive dissonance*. Your beliefs, behaviors, and attitude are inconsistent—or, to express it more simply, you say one thing and do another. Dissonance is another way of saying unbalanced, and the more it persists, the more uncomfortable and miserable we become.

To discuss the concept of cognitive dissonance further, I reached out to my friend Daven Morrison, a board-certified psychiatrist with Morrison Associates, Ltd., who works closely with companies and executives on areas related to decision-making and performance. Daven explained that the fundamental function of the brain is to find and match patterns, which helps make life predictable: sunrise to sunset, summer changing into winter. We see an object—say something as simple as a pencil or a candle—and we know from past experience how it works. But if we come across one of those trick birthday candles that you can't blow out, it doesn't match our expectation of how the world is supposed to work. The result is a kind of cognitive dissonance.

On a more dramatic scale, a natural disaster such as an earthquake or a tornado can rock our world: we go from a calm and predictable day to devastation a few hours later. But even then, Daven said, the human mind is able to recover more quickly from the shock of a natural disaster than when we're betrayed by another person. In the same way, when someone we admire and whom we think of as leading a values-based life does something unethical or illegal, Daven said, "it shakes the ground we stand on."

Although outside events and the behaviors of others can upset us, we also bring it on ourselves when our actions are inconsistent with our values. Complicating matters, humans have the capacity to rationalize just about anything. For example, in his studies of white-collar crime and fraud, Daven discovered that many people say they intended to pay back the money they took, which to their mind meant they didn't see it as stealing. Others felt they were justified—they were "owed" more than they received. They'd never describe themselves as greedy. And there can be group dynamics that encourage and ingrain behaviors that would usually be unthinkable for the individual.

Unethical and criminal behaviors are extreme examples of actions that conflict with our values. On a less dramatic scale, there are many things we do every day that are out of alignment. A simple example is when we say that we value being healthy—we want to exercise more and eat better. We put on exercise clothes to go to the gym, but instead head over to a fast food restaurant for a double burger and an extra-large order of fries. Afterward, there is bound to be rationalization and bargaining with one's self ("Tomorrow I'll work out twice as much.") and probably some shame and guilt. Even addictions, infidelity, and other serious behavioral issues can get rationalized away: "if no one knows, no one gets hurt." That results in a guaranteed collision between what someone is telling themselves and what will happen when their behaviors are discovered.

Cognitive dissonance can even take root in our concept of time. We have an unrealistic expectation of all that we can do in one day. One young professional described her life as working two jobs, going to school, spending time with friends, and enjoying leisure activities. After a few weeks, reality hit—and hard. She was exhausted and upset and couldn't figure out what had gone wrong. Had she counted the number of hours for each activity and plotted them into the 168-hour life grid, she'd see that her view of the world required a 185-hour week—not reality!

The solution is self-reflection. Otherwise, it will be very difficult to see where and how you're out of alignment with your values. You simply won't recognize when your life is inconsistent with your values. It may be that you aren't sure what your values are. Or, even if you have a loose concept of what's most important, you're not really comfortable with the kind of self-examination it takes to be honest with yourself. A case in point: the average person knows that each of us is going to die. Yet a study by AARP found that 60 percent of people have no will or estate planning.[2] Self-awareness, then, is the only way to reduce imbalance, live in alignment with our values, and stay grounded in reality.

This type of reflection brings up profound, existential questions that call for deeper evaluation of how we spend our time. "Is my life meaningful? Am I making a difference—and if so, how?" "These are difficult questions to talk through," Daven said. "When we think about our end of life, it's hard to look at it."

For some people, the response may be to recoil from these tough questions. They'd rather push aside worries over whether they should change their health habits or address an addiction. But for others, it can be a wake-up call to examine the reality of how and where they spend their time and the dissonance between their words and actions.

"With existential things, we're usually so uncomfortable with the question that we are only aware of the tip of the iceberg, and so we address our worry superficially—for example, through exercise or working harder. Yet sometimes the discomfort does not go away just by working in this way. When this happens, there's something deeper going on—a root cause tied to questions we may not be able to fully answer," Daven said. "The real work is understanding what is possible to understand and coming to peace with what we cannot. Daily reflection and deeper self-reflection in general help with this distress by reminding us of what we believe in, that we're not alone, and that others we love and care about will carry on in meaningful ways and with our influence."

The more each of us is willing to question what's really going on and how we really feel, the more likely we'll stay true to our values and continue to be guided by our moral compass.

To engage in this type of self-examination, you must take time by yourself to reflect on the deep and probing questions. As I discussed in chapter 1, you must also seek the input and perspective of valued, trusted people whose values match yours. And, as we discuss in chapter 3, you may benefit from a supportive community for making positive changes in your life. But it always comes back to you.

What that looks like is up to each individual. One person's choices will be different from another's. That doesn't make one person right and another wrong. Balance can only come from being true to ourselves by making choices that are authentic to us and our priorities, with the self-awareness of the likely outcome or consequences.

When I think of Bill, the executive I knew many years ago, it was clear in our conversations that he wasn't self-reflective. He was looking for me to give him some quick-fix advice—like taking the family on a vacation or other check-the-box activities. He wasn't willing to sit down and ask himself what his values were and what mattered most to him. If he had, he would be able to make choices for himself that enabled him to have the life he wanted—whether that meant more or less golf, more or less family time, or anything else. He needed to figure out what was really most important. If that was golf, then he'd have to own that and be honest with himself. Because he said he wanted to have a stronger relationship with his family, however, he needed to take a look at how he was spending his 168 hours a week.

WHEN LIFE GETS COMPLICATED

I don't know anybody who has a simple life. For most of us, it's complicated. We're juggling a million things, and some of those things are really big responsibilities—like children. I know from experience just how challenging it can be for a two-career couple with children to figure out how to balance everything without being surprised.

When Julie and I had our first child, Suzie, we were both working full-time. We didn't make enough money to hire live-in help, so when Julie went back to work, we decided to take Suzie to day care. This required a lot of coordination. Our solution was to be really planful to keep things running as smoothly as possible. Self-reflection also helped identify what *could* go wrong so we could have a contingency plan. We needed to know what we would do when something occurred so we wouldn't be panicked and scrambling. In other words, we didn't want to be surprised—especially because at the center of that surprise would be our child!

Every day, Julie and I knew who was dropping Suzie off at day care at seven-thirty in the morning and who was going to pick her up at five-thirty. Sometimes that was Julie and sometimes that was me. But there were times when neither of us could pick up Suzie—flights were delayed, we were stuck at work. When that happened, we didn't panic because we knew *ahead of time* what we would do: we contacted a good friend of ours who had agreed well in advance to be our backup. If neither Julie nor I could get to the day care by five-thirty, our friend was there.

I can't think of a better example of the importance of planning ahead and knowing what you'd do if things don't go as planned. You can't afford to pretend that nothing will ever go wrong. Believe me, when you're sitting in LaGuardia Airport and your flight is delayed three hours, you don't want to wonder who is going to pick up your child at day care.

As I said, we are works in progress. Sometimes, even when we're planful, things get complicated—like when our second child, Andrew, was born. Julie had taken off two months for maternity leave and then returned to her job. On her first day back to work, I took both three-year-old Suzie and two-month-old Andrew to day care.

It was a routine for me by this time: go to day care, drop off Suzie, go to the office. On this particular morning, I had to give a presentation to the board of directors. I parked my car at the office and grabbed my briefcase. Just then I noticed Andrew was still in the back, in his car seat. (And yes, I was surprised.)

I had been so used to dropping off Suzie, I completely forgot I was now dropping off two children. By this time, Andrew was starting to cry. I called my assistant and explained that someone else was going to have to make the first presentation at the board meeting. I had to go back to Evanston to drop off Andrew.

When I arrived, the woman who ran the day care was waiting for me at the door. "I was wondering when you would realize that Andrew was in the back seat of your car."

I still get teased about that one.

The message here is life gets complicated and we have to rebalance constantly. There are new projects at work, issues with the children, elderly parents who need more care. No matter how well we plan, life throws us curve balls. We have to be ready to take on those things that can and will go wrong by being self-reflective and self-aware.

SURPRISES WON'T WAIT UNTIL IT'S CONVENIENT

In my classes when I discuss the importance of being self-reflective to minimize the surprises, there are always students who tell me that they're going to approach it differently. Their plan is to work as hard as they can for the first few years after graduation, make as much money as possible, and then they can ease up and get things in balance. Often, these are the students who are entertaining one of those job offers that involves 90-hour weeks and constant travel.

This is nothing new: I've seen my peers try the same thing. But if you're not self-aware, it can result in a series of problems. So before they sign up, my advice is that they think about several things. First, how will that align with their life right now? If they plan to get married and have children (not everyone does), then how will intense job pressure affect their family life?

The second issue is how long they intend to work as hard as they can. Two years? Three? What happens if it turns into five or ten? The problem is once you turn it on, it's hard to turn off. You get promoted, the money is good, and it's hard to step away. Now, if that's what you really want, then go for it. Just make sure that you self-reflect on your choices so you won't be surprised. Your life buckets are going to look different from other people's, and the biggest bucket is going to be your work. It's like people who are all in on one aspect of their lives—training for the Olympics, trying to make it to the big time as a musician or other performer. These pursuits will consume a very big part of their 168 hours a week, with little room left over. The same is true for those road warrior consultants who leave home first thing Monday morning (and sometimes Sunday night) and are lucky if they get to come home Thursday night and work in their home office on Friday. Then, a few days later, it's back on the road again.

If you want to do that (or feel you have to do that) for the money or to build your career, then understand the sacrifices you're going to make. There is nothing wrong with that as long as you know the implications and avoid surprises later. However, it's a very real risk—I've seen it among recent graduates and my peers. Even if your personal relationships stay intact, the fact is you won't be around very much. You'll miss birthdays and family parties. If you decide to have children, your baby's first steps will be recorded on a smartphone and sent to you. No judgment here—just be aware of the trade-offs so that you're not surprised.

Now here's the third point. Let's say you have reached the point in your career when you can slow down or take a step back.

You have one problem: how do you do that? Are all those things that weren't important to you for three or five years suddenly important? You missed your daughter's soccer games from first through third grades, so what is going to make the fourth-grade soccer games more engaging for you? And what about your daughter? She knows you weren't there for the first three years, so if you're suddenly at the field for every practice and game, she'll wonder what's going on. Will she really want you there?

NO AGE LIMIT ON SURPRISES

When it comes to being surprised, there's no age limit. You can be blindsided at 80 just as you can at 18. And the reason is the same: a lack of self-reflection. Although self-reflection is a habit you can adopt at any age, there is a big advantage to getting into the habit when you're young. The younger you are when you begin practicing self-reflection, the more surprises you can avoid in your life.

One student I know graduated with a music performance degree from a well-regarded music conservatory and gave himself a year to decide what to do next. When that year was up, he didn't have a plan, so he decided to go to graduate school by default. He went to the only school that accepted him. Needless to say, it was not the greatest experience, didn't help his career, and added to his significant student debt. Had he been self-reflective, he probably would have made choices that were proactive and not just reactive. Most likely he would have realized that he needed input from some trusted advisors whose values and priorities were aligned with his to help him figure it out. Instead, he's right back where he was after getting his undergraduate degree: no professional job and no real plan.

Among middle-aged people, I've noticed that a lot of the surprises are on the home front. Once people get into their mid-40s and are doing well in their careers, they immediately decide it's time for that big house with six bedrooms. Every time you talk to them, they're meeting with architects and contractors to build that dream home—which is fast on its way to becoming a nightmare. It takes twice as long to build and costs way more than they budgeted. But finally it's done and the family moves in.

Flash forward about a decade. The kids are out of the house and there they are, two people in a place that's just too big. Now they want to sell that house. You have to wonder: didn't they realize, ten years ago, that their children were going to grow up and go out on their own? Apparently not, because every time they see that for sale sign on the lawn, they're surprised.

This type of thinking never stops. Many of my friends from high school, college, and graduate school are thinking about retirement. In the last few months before they stop working, they don't talk about anything other than how they can't wait to retire. Then they'll have all the time in the world to do everything they've ever wanted to do.

So what happens? Immediately after retiring, they take a month-long trip and then, when they come home, they play golf every day for two weeks. And then it's Monday morning. That's what happened to Sam, who announced to his wife, Jean, that now they could have lunch together every day.

Jean, however, had news for Sam: "You know, I've gotten used to not having lunch with you for 35 years. You being home for lunch now will be incredibly inconvenient for me."

For all those years when Sam was going 100 miles an hour in his job, he never really thought about what he would do when he retired. When retirement was on the horizon, he never put together a plan for volunteering or taking up a hobby. He had no plan at all. Now that he's retired, he has no idea what to do for the next 20 or 30 years and, to him, it's actually very surprising.

NEXT STEPS TO BETTER BALANCE

If you've been surprised in your life—or, maybe, if you're surprised right now—embrace it as a wake-up call. Now that you're aware, take some time to ask yourself, "Why am I surprised?" In hindsight, is this something you could have foreseen and potentially avoided? As you engage in self-examination, you'll realize the tremendous benefit of being self-reflective to minimize the chances that you'll be surprised in the future.

In this exercise, create a life grid (see table 2.1) of where you spend your time now versus how you'd like to allocate time in your life buckets. As you examine the goals and actual hours spent, what changes do you want to make to get more in balance? (Note: life bucket categories should reflect what matters most to *you*.)

Table 2.1   *Examine the goals and hours spent in your life buckets.*

Life Bucket	Goal Hours	Actual Hours Spent	Difference
Career			
Family			
Faith/Spirituality			
Health/Sleep			
Fun/Recreation/ Reading			
Making a Difference			
	168 hours (100%)		

CHAPTER 3

HITTING THE BRICK WALL

When surprises go unheeded, they don't just fade away. Without the self-awareness that comes from self-reflection, a relatively minor surprise or small problem compounds into a major upset. Now you've got a full-blown crisis on your hands. As I've seen among people I know, including those who have shared their life journeys with me, these crises often spill over into numerous areas: a major relationship is in turmoil, someone's health suffers, a job is in jeopardy. Maybe this has happened to you or to someone you know. If so, then you understand that hitting the brick wall can cause wreckage everywhere in your life.

The best course of action is prevention: self-reflection (see chapter 1) and paying attention to surprises (see chapter 2). But we're all works in progress. We're never in balance all the time, and unfortunately, sometimes it can be too easy to ignore what's happening in our lives. Or we pay attention to a surprise for a little while, adjusting our behaviors and trying to be more balanced. But we don't stick to it and soon go back to our old ways. It's as if we realize that going 90 miles an hour on the highway is not sustainable and we get off at the next exit ramp. The problem is it's so easy to take the next on-ramp onto that highway, and then it's as if we never slowed down at all.

When we're not self-reflective, we can convince ourselves that "things aren't that bad" or "that's just the way it is." We'll address a problem or issue tomorrow—but right now, we're just too busy, stressed, and moving too fast. We become immune to surprises and far too adept at self-deception.

Perhaps becoming extremely unbalanced in your life has occurred so gradually, you did not really notice it happening. Unknowingly, you detoured further and further from what you thought your life would look like, and now you're not even aware that you're just wandering around. You may be lost without even realizing it.

FOLLOWING OTHERS INTO TROUBLE

Here's a story from my childhood in Pennsylvania that I use to illustrate the danger of what can happen if you're not really aware. One hot summer, I went with my friends to the city pool. I was only in second grade at the time, but because I was pretty good at baseball, my friends in fifth and sixth grade would let me play with them. The age and size difference on the baseball field may not have been as noticeable, but in the pool, it quickly became undeniable.

The shallow end of the pool was roughly two feet deep. We started there and walked toward the deep end. One day, I followed my friends as they headed to deeper water. Soon I was over my head. I was trying to stand in six feet of water, but instead I was sinking. I couldn't swim—and I couldn't breathe, either!

Looking up through the water, I could see a lifeguard on a stand at the side of the pool. I started waving to get her attention. At first, she waved back, so I waved more frantically. Thankfully, she realized what was going on, dove into the water, and pulled me out. "What were you doing?" she asked me.

"I was just walking with my friends," I told her. It never really occurred to me that they were two feet taller than I was so they could walk (and swim) into deeper water where I just couldn't go. The point of this story is that it can be so easy to gradually continue what you're doing without noticing the risks—until suddenly, you're in over your head.

Although my swimming pool story certainly isn't meant to put any blame on my childhood baseball buddies, it does remind us that we can follow other people into trouble. Sometimes, a friend is a bad influence in adopting behaviors that undermine your values. Other times, it can be a classic case of socializing with people who make you feel inadequate. You try to keep up with the Joneses, such as with a bigger house, a nicer car, or designer clothing. But it's a moving target. We buy a BMW, but our neighbor now drives a Mercedes. We trade up for a Mercedes, but now the neighbor is behind the wheel of a Rolls-Royce. The name for this is *conspicuous consumption*, which we may associate with the 1980s and the status bestowed by owning (and wearing) certain brands. But conspicuous consumption is a sociological and socioeconomic concept that dates back to the late 19th century. It describes US consumer behavior to express culture and values through the goods one purchases. (Hint: these kinds of "values" are not the basis of a values-based life.) More recently, mounting household debt has been directly linked to the lure of conspicuous consumption and the desire to keep up with the Joneses. It doesn't matter that one group does not have the same earning power as the group they try to emulate. The income inequality leads to more consumer borrowing, researchers say, as "households with smaller income gains … use debt to keep up their consumption level relative to households with larger income gains."[1]

In what I've witnessed, the Joneses effect isn't limited to people who are trying to pass themselves off as wealthier than they are. Among the top tier of wealthy individuals, there can be fierce competition for who has the most impressive possessions.

I witnessed this firsthand several years ago when I, as CEO of Baxter International, was invited to participate in a business forum that brought together some of the largest global companies. At a dinner, I was seated between two CEOs who I won't name except to tell you they had one commonality: a few years later, both would be in the headlines for allegations of corporate fraud and Securities and Exchange Commission investigations into misleading investors. Both were convicted and faced prison sentences.

None of that had happened at the time of this dinner. But with one on my left and one on my right, I was in the middle of their small talk about construction of their third or fourth homes and problems with their Lamborghinis and Ferraris. Finally, I piped up. "My Honda Accord is still running really well." They looked at me as if I were from Mars. For them, it was just how they were keeping score. My Honda and I were clearly not part of that game.

People laugh when I tell this story, but there's a sobering truth here. Without self-reflection, it's so easy to be tempted by money and what it can buy. It's not that money is bad—it's a resource and should be treated as such. But as your success increases and with it your income, you can be tempted to keep score like those CEOs at dinner, until you convince yourself that you want and truly do need something bigger, better, flashier, and more expensive.

Again, the vacation house or fancy sports car, in and of itself, won't undermine your values. If you are truly passionate about cars, for example, and driving one is a big part of your leisure bucket (perhaps an interest that you share with family and friends), then enjoy! Just be self-reflective about what and why you're buying something. As my father always reminded me, "Harry, never allow yourself to be possessed by your possessions."

A friend of mine told me a story about a couple who appeared to have everything: the beautiful house in the "right" suburb, the fanciest cars, the most exquisite designer clothes that the couple loved to show off whenever they entertained or traveled. But their business was hit hard during the 2008–2009 financial crisis. With their income only a fraction of what it had been previously, the man secretly took on huge amounts of debt to keep up the façade of wealth and privilege. It was not sustainable, and when the bank repossessed their house, the truth was finally exposed. Even though he said his motivation was to maintain his wife's lifestyle, she was so infuriated by this deception that she divorced him. He lost his house, possessions, and marriage all because of an attempt to maintain appearances.

We can imagine that, at some point before their circumstances hit the crisis point, there were indications that all was not as it seemed. Maybe a credit card was declined when a purchase was being made. Or there was a scramble to get another loan. These "surprises" could have been a wake-up call that may have enabled this couple to face reality together. Whatever the reason, that did not happen. When this couple hit the brick wall, everything shattered.

THE FORK IN THE ROAD

The brick wall will look different, depending on a person's circumstances or situation. Maybe someone has gained a significant amount of weight, increasing their health risks—even to the point of suffering a heart attack at an early age. Maybe someone's significant other announced that he or she is tired of broken promises and excuses and has just delivered an ultimatum. Negative behaviors may also be threatening someone's career to the point they're afraid of losing their job—or may have already lost it.

Or maybe the job is the problem. What started out at 40 hours a week has escalated to the point that now someone is working 80, 90, even 100 hours a week. It's been easy to rationalize because she's so successful in her work bucket. But maybe now it's 15 years into her career, and she has neglected both family and friends. Her 40th birthday arrives and she decides to throw a party but gets no response because people haven't heard from her in so long.

Sometimes the brick wall can come in the form of confrontation with a loved one, who demands to know why you've been missing from their lives. There's no ultimatum, no loss of love or support—just a frank question, "Why aren't you here?"

The first few times this question gets asked, the answer or explanation may seem straightforward: you're busy at work. Your job demands have increased. Your boss expects you to travel most of the time for your work. You really don't have a choice.

When the question "Why aren't you here?" is asked again and again, those simple answers won't satisfy anyone. Your spouse, partner, children, or other loved ones want to know when you are going to stop being absent. It's a hard question. Walking away from job demands may not be possible given your financial circumstances. Working full-time and going to school may have put you out of balance more than you expected.

As I tell my students, I don't have any answers, but I do have opinions. If any of these stories and examples resonate with you, then you've gone beyond merely being surprised. You're at or near the brick wall. Now you have two choices. The first is you can try to ignore what is happening in your life. It may seem to work for a little while. But when personal or family relationships are in jeopardy, your health risks have escalated considerably, or addictions are overtaking your life, denial will only take you further down a destructive path. At some point, being surprised won't even be an option. Instead, you'll be confronted by an even bigger brick wall.

The second choice is you can respond with significant changes. Often, these changes are so profound that they amount to self-disrupting your life. In fact, the only way back toward balance is with changes that are of the same magnitude as the brick wall you just hit. Your response may involve counseling or a 12-step program. You may quit your job or change jobs. You may have to make radical changes to your diet and lifestyle to improve your health. You may have to move out of the house you can't afford and sell the cars with payments that are beyond your budget.

Whatever you decide, if you truly want to improve your life and commit to the pursuit of better balance in how you allocate your 168, then your response needs to catapult you out of your routine. Maybe you go off for a weekend retreat, start seeing a counselor, or even hike in the desert. It needs to be enough of a disruptive experience that you change the status quo and pull yourself out of deep habits that are difficult to change.

THE SELF-DISRUPTED LIFE

My friend and colleague Carter Cast has an impressive resume: a former marketing executive for several iconic consumer brands, chief marketing officer of an e-commerce jewelry company, and CEO of a major online retailer. Today he is a clinical professor of innovation and entrepreneurship at Kellogg and also a venture partner for a major venture capital group. In addition, he's a husband, father, and author of a best-selling book, *The Right (and Wrong) Stuff: How Brilliant Careers Are Made and Unmade.* What I admire most about Carter is his decision to self-disrupt his life. It's an inspiring story he shares with candor.

Carter's brick wall was health-related. He was 30 pounds overweight, had heart arrhythmia, and needed to have stomach surgery to address debilitating acid reflux. He hadn't exercised in longer than he could remember, which was unthinkable for this former college All-American swimmer. He had lost touch with most of his friends and could no longer deny that "when you don't reach out to them, they stop calling you." The problem was his career, which consumed more and more of his time, to the point he was exhausted and burned out. He still managed to hang in there with immediate family, including his wife and children. But he could no longer avoid an uncomfortable truth. As Carter recalled, "I didn't like who I had become."

Carter had gone beyond being surprised. He'd hit a brick wall.

His response to this massive wake-up call was what he called a time-out. "I benched myself," he said. He quit his job and simplified his lifestyle. What followed was a prolonged period of self-reflection and self-examination. "I had to create a disruptive experience to get out of the groove of my bad lifestyle," Carter recalled.

Looking back, Carter drew from author William Bridges to describe the three phases of the transition that took him from a burned-out executive to a clinical professor and venture capital partner—with much greater awareness of the importance of balance in his life. The phases are endings, neutral zones, and beginnings.

Phase 1: Marking the End

The ending phase is when you finally decide to put an end to what caused you to hit the brick wall. This was the time-out that occurred for Carter after he hit the brick wall. He stopped working countless hours and ignoring the impact on his health.

Taking this step is momentous and brave. Admittedly, some people may not be able to quit their jobs as Carter did. But even if you're the main breadwinner of your family and you're working too many hours or the stress of your job is affecting your health and your relationships, you need to find a way to take some time off. A weekend retreat may give you the mental space to see things more clearly and start contemplating changes that will bring your life out of crisis and into better balance.

It's no use trying to convince yourself that you can change while you continue with the same routines that smashed you into the brick wall. Something has to change! As Carter noted, "There's a saying that when you're doing a trapeze act, you have to let go of one trapeze swing in order to catch the other one. You must let go to move forward. It was the same thing with my life transition—I needed a clean and clear ending to be able to move forward."

His suggestion is to mark the ending with a ritual of some type to help you close the door. "Maybe you burn an old picture of yourself. Or you cut your hair off. Whatever it is, you acknowledge to yourself that this is an end. From here, it's a new way forward."

Phase 2: Entering the Neutral Zone

When one thing ends, you don't rush to fill the gap. Instead, you enter a transitional time called the *neutral zone*. This is where you investigate, explore, and try on different roles to see what might fit you and your sense of purpose and help you create a more balanced life.

For Carter, the neutral zone was a two-year period during which he gave himself permission to try on different roles. As he explained, "I was testing different identities to see what fits." For Carter, that meant he was doing some consulting—not jumping in to become a consultant. It meant doing some educational administration work—not jumping into a full-time staff role in education. "I was trying on clothes, wearing them around and seeing how they fit, how I felt in them," he said. Carter tried some teaching before he was ready to announce he had become a teacher.

Thanks to experimentation in the neutral zone, Carter could keep an open mind to experience what worked for him and what didn't. For example, he tried corporate consulting but didn't relish a role that involved mostly (as he put it) "interviewing people and then making recommendations—that didn't feel like me. I'm a doer by nature." He tried on the executive director role at Kellogg's Innovation and Entrepreneurship Initiative, but that didn't suit him, either.

Just because a role didn't fit didn't make it a failure. Instead, Carter cited a quote by Thomas Edison, who persevered through many iterations until he finally perfected the lightbulb. As Edison said, "I have not failed. I've just found 10,000 ways that won't work."

Carter had a far different experience with teaching: first as a guest lecturer, then co-teaching a class, teaching a class, and teaching multiple classes. Similarly, when he was approached by the Pritzker Group, a Chicago-based venture capital firm, he was open to explore what this might entail because he was passionate about entrepreneurship. It started with a conversation with J. B. Pritzker, cofounder of the Pritzker Group (and, today, governor of Illinois) about his background and whether he'd be open to advising a company or two for them. Carter agreed, and when that went well, he started to advise more companies and became a strategic advisor for three months. Then, just as happened for him with teaching, his interest in entrepreneurship and venture capital increased over time, until he became a venture partner.

Over time, he expanded his experimentation and, at one point, was doing several different jobs. Finally, he settled on a path that embraced his roles of "husband, father, son, brother, teacher, writer/speaker, venture capitalist, and community citizen." Each of these roles is closely aligned with his sense of purpose and reinforces the pursuit of balance in his life.

Phase 3: Marking the Beginning

Through testing and experimentation, the pieces will come together to help you create a values-based life. It is a process and can't be rushed. The experimental nature of the neutral zone reinforces humility—you don't have the immediate answers. (You just hit a brick wall, remember?) Instead, you remain open, engage in continuous self-reflection, and seek the advice of others—both trusted people in your life (as mentioned in chapter 2) as well as inspiring books that provide insight into how you can create a values-based life.

When you know what you will do with your time and talent going forward, you can mark a new beginning. Hope that you are not the same as you were at the start of this process. You know more about yourself and you're building new habits (as we discuss in chapter 4) that will literally ingrain new behaviors.

For Carter, the neutral zone ended in 2012, and he entered a new beginning with teaching and working in venture capital, along with reading, study, exercise, and greater self-awareness. After quitting his job, he enjoyed more time to read, and he devoured countless books on religion, spirituality, and philosophy, as well as literature. "I fell in love with wisdom and knowledge, and became so appreciative of the great thinkers and their influence on my life," explained Carter, who related it to the famous quote by Sir Isaac Newton: "If I have seen further it is by standing on the shoulders of giants."

He began journaling about what he was reading and absorbing to the point he filled up 22 journals and then summarized (and later digitized) the journals for easier access and ability to cross-reference the insights. Through this process of reading and journaling, Carter developed a system he called *notes to myself*, which codifies how he wants to approach life and the person he strives to become.

WHAT WILL THE NEIGHBORS THINK?

If pursuing wealth, possessions, and status has put you on the collision course with the brick wall, making changes will probably become complicated for you by a nagging fear: "What will the neighbors [or family or friends or peers] think?" We assign these people so much influence, as if their opinions matter very much to us. Often the thinking goes something like this: "I can't quite possibly quit my job, because what will So-and-So think? I know I can't afford my house and I have to get out from under this debt, but if a 'for sale' sign goes up tomorrow, what will the neighbors think? If I decide that I don't want to be a [insert current occupation] any longer, and instead I want to be a [insert new occupation], what will my family think?"

This thinking becomes a vicious cycle, and suddenly you are more worried about other people's opinions instead of leading a more authentic, values-based life. Here's the good news: your family and friends who really love you and want the best for you are probably going to be supportive of the changes you want to make in your life. After all, they've seen you be surprised, and they may have witnessed you hitting the brick wall. So, when you tell them that you've gone through the three phases of ending, the neutral zone, and beginning, they'll most likely be happy for you. Their biggest concern for you is whether you're taking care of yourself. Although they're proud of you, they are most concerned about whether you're really happy and able to keep your life in perspective.

The neighbors, acquaintances, former classmates, and colleagues simply are not thinking about you as much as you imagine (and probably they're not thinking of you at all). They've got their own problems to think about—their mortgages, health, marriages, and job performance, as well as the surprises that are getting their attention. So don't let someone else's opinion (real or imagined) keep you from living the life that is right for you.

All too often, people stray from becoming their true selves and living a values-based life out of fear of what others think of them. A story that has always illustrated this point for me was of a man I met in a nursing home many years ago. To explain, after my parents retired in Minnesota, they decided to give back to their community by volunteering at nursing homes in the Minneapolis–St. Paul area. My father liked to sing, and my mother played the piano, so they gave several performances every month for nursing home residents. I tried to attend their shows on my frequent visits to Minnesota.

On one occasion, I sat next to a gentleman in his late eighties. I'll never forget how elegantly he was dressed, in a handsome tweed jacket and a bow tie. As my parents performed, he hummed along to the song "Oklahoma." After the performance, as the cake and coffee were served, I started talking to the man. He told me he had been a senior executive at Pillsbury, which prompted me to ask him several questions about his life experiences: why he had made certain decisions and what he might have done differently. I'll never forget his answer. When he was in his forties, he seriously considered leaving the corporate world and becoming a teacher, but ultimately decided against it. "The reason I didn't do it was because I was worried about what 'they' would think," he told me. "You know what? I'm 89 years old now, and I spend a lot of my time thinking about things. Who were 'those people' I was so worried about, and why did I care so much about what they thought?"

The moral of this story is that focusing too much on the opinions of others can lead you right into a brick wall. Instead, you must be comfortable with yourself and who you really are, and make choices that support leading a values-based life. Or as Carter says, quoting one of his favorite mantras, "Your opinion of me is none of my business."

IT TAKES TIME TO RECOVER

Imagine for a moment that you're driving on an icy road. You're in a hurry, you're not paying as much attention as you should, and you're tired and distracted. You hit black ice, the car spins out of control, and you slam into the concrete wall. Your car is totaled, and you have some injuries—your arm is broken, you have whiplash, and even though the airbag deployed, you may have hit your head as the car spun around. You're transported to the hospital by ambulance.

Do you think you would wave off the ambulance, call an Uber instead, and immediately go to the nearest car dealership so you can get right back on the road? Not likely. In fact, you're probably shaken up by what just happened and realizing just how much worse it could have been.

The same applies when you hit a figurative wall in your life. You were going too fast, didn't notice the hazards, ignored the surprises, were distracted and exhausted, and totaled your life (or at least parts of it). Recovering is going to take time and patience. Transitioning from the way you were living to having the values-based life you truly want is not instantaneous. You need to self-reflect and seek the input of others.

As we discuss in chapter 4, taking those first steps of building new habits and creating values-based routines will require effort and repetition. Plus, you'll be doing a lot of experimenting along the way as you discover more about yourself and who you want to become.

We can find lessons and reminders all around us—in nature, where it takes time for a seed to germinate and the plant to grow, for a caterpillar to change into a butterfly, and for the seasons to transition from one to the next. If you become impatient or easily discouraged, you will set yourself up for disappointment and failure. You can't leapfrog ahead, from deciding you want to be more involved in your community to deciding that next month you're going to be running an NGO. The transition to your best self takes time, slowly changing and building a life that is authentic and sustainable. If you are willing to accept and understand these truths, then you will enjoy the journey and the process. With continual self-reflection, you'll discover and create a values-based life.

NEXT STEPS TO BETTER BALANCE

If you hit the wall, or you've gotten dangerously close, then consider it a wake-up call to take action and self-disrupt your life.

Although it's unrealistic for most people to instantly quit their job and take an extended time-out, it is still possible to step outside your routines and ingrained habits so you can gain clarity and perspective. Consider the following:

- A weekend retreat to ponder your purpose and values
- A day (or two) away—in the woods, at the beach, or other change of scenery
- Several hours of meaningful time by yourself—someplace quiet and free of distractions
- Unplug from your devices—leave the phone, tablet, and so on at home; eliminate the noise

As you carve out time for yourself, here are some questions to ponder:

- Where and how have I hit the wall?
- In retrospect, what surprises did I ignore that led to a bigger problem or even a crisis?
- Has comparing myself to others and keeping up with the Joneses led me away from my values?
- Am I ready to change—even to the point of self-disruption? If so, what changes would I like to test out?
- What are the things I've always wanted to do but didn't pursue because I was too afraid of what other people would think?
- What do I want my values-based life to look like going forward?

CHAPTER 4

BUILDING NEW HABITS

Every year, several students in my Kellogg classes embrace self-reflection and its importance in reducing surprises, and their response is "sign me up! I'm ready to change." They have good intentions. They understand that self-reflection is essential to living a values-based life. They acknowledge how often they've been surprised in the past, and they want to prevent that from happening as much as possible. They dive in, with plans to make dramatic changes.

One student, James, told me recently that he was committed to *an hour* of self-reflection every day. No matter that he had never before engaged in self-reflection as a regular practice, or that 15 minutes is what I recommend at the start; he wanted a big change. As he saw it, if 15 minutes was beneficial, then an hour was going to be four time more effective. "By next week," he told me enthusiastically, "you're going to see an enormous change in me."

When I saw James in class the following week, I could tell by the disappointed look on his face that things hadn't gone as planned. "The first two days I managed to do an hour of self-reflection, but after that I just couldn't keep doing it. By the fourth day, I had stopped reflecting completely," he admitted. "I am very disappointed in myself."

My students are top achievers and very goal-oriented, and James is no exception. He's used to accomplishing whatever he puts his mind to, whether that's getting an A in class or performing extremely well in a job interview. Compared to those achievements, he thought, how hard could it be to sit for an hour each day and ponder deep questions about life? He failed—and he was surprised. "I should be able to do this," he told me, "but I don't think I can."

What James didn't count on was how hard it is to adopt a new, regular habit. To engage in self-reflection for an hour a day, he had to reallocate his time. He decided to wake up an hour earlier every day and change his morning routine. That turned out to be more challenging than he expected. His old habits of sleeping as late as possible or watching the morning news tempted him away from his new habit of self-reflection.

As I explained to James, habits don't turn on and off with a switch. You can't assume that you'll immediately adopt a new habit, consistently and sustainably, any more than a brand-new driver can go from a standstill in a parking lot to driving 70 miles an hour down the freeway. For James, going from zero self-reflection to an hour a day was too much to expect of himself.

HABITS ARE HARD TO BREAK—AND BUILD

James's disappointment explains why about 80 percent of New Year's resolutions are said to fail by mid-February—and why so many gym membership sign-ups in January end up with cancellations a month or two later. Our old habits are harder to break than we realize. In addition, we don't have as much time as we think we do, even for something that we truly want to start doing. For example, let's say you want to take up the piano. You convince yourself that you can commit to weekly lessons and practice an hour a day, even though you're working 50 hours a week, traveling for business, and have a family. In your eagerness to add this enriching experience, you convince yourself that you can make time—as if you can squeeze piano practice into hours 169, 170, and 171 for the week.

It's so easy to forget the reality of your 168. That's all the time we have, and everything from sleeping to working to exercising to spending time with family and enjoying leisure activities can only consume 168 hours a week—and not a minute more.

The reality of 168 means that for every activity you add, something else has to change. You'll be doing less of a longtime habit or else drop it completely. You decide to go back to school, which means night classes and homework will consume the time you used to spend watching your favorite media and playing video games. Intellectually you may say, "Well, that's a better use of my time." No matter what you tell yourself, though, in practice it will prove more difficult than you expect. Neuroscience tells us why that is.

Habits, both good and bad, are patterns that over time become etched onto our neural pathways. That's why it's so hard for an old pattern, with its well-formed neural pathway, to be replaced with a new one. We may be conscious of all the valid reasons why we should adopt a new behavior, but our brain patterns lead us in a different direction—and often right back to our old habit. If that ingrained pattern is to sleep as late as possible then race to work while eating a doughnut, it's going to take quite a bit of time and effort to adopt the new habit of getting out of bed and immediately going to the gym.

Triggers and cues—things we associate with certain behaviors—also reinforce our habits. For example, a man I know, George, had a cigarette with his morning coffee every day for 40 years. It was a habit he enjoyed, and no amount of awareness of the health risks of smoking could convince him he should try (again) to quit. Then one day George ended up in the intensive care unit with a severe health issue, and the doctors told him he could never smoke again. As he wrapped his mind around the urgency of adopting a new behavior, George couldn't imagine drinking coffee without having a cigarette. Although he never thought about one being a cue or a trigger for the other, George just knew that those two habits—coffee and a cigarette—went together. Fortunately, George was able to break the habit, but it was very difficult as he struggled at first. Eventually, he formed a new neural pathway: morning coffee with the newspaper and without the cigarette.

The good news, as George's experience shows us, is that habits can be changed. We can eliminate unwanted behaviors and adopt new ones that better reflect our values. The key is repetition until new neural pathways become etched like a groove in a vinyl record. But it takes time. As Charles Duhigg wrote in *The Power of Habit: Why We Do What We Do in Life and Business*, "Transforming a habit isn't necessarily easy or quick. It isn't always simple. But it is possible."[1]

The cornerstone for any change is continuous self-reflection. In my own life, that's how I identify habits I want to change, select new behaviors I want to adopt, and keep myself accountable. I reflect on how I am going to accomplish it, whether something is realistic given my 168, and how well I'm doing in changing a behavior and adopting a hew habit. Most important, I reflect on how this new or additional habit will enhance my values-based life.

Let's start there. As you look at your life buckets of how and where you want to allocate your 168 hours a week, where do you want to make changes? Are you looking to spend more time with family and loved ones? Do you want to exercise more, eat healthier, or get more sleep? Are you looking to change what you do for leisure? My suggestion is to start with *one life bucket* and consciously identify one or two new behaviors or habits that you want to adopt so that the life you're living is more aligned with your values. Trying to do too much all at once will only lead to frustration and a setback. Instead, approach this new habit as a process. There's a lot of work ahead, but the payoff of leading a values-based life is very rewarding.

SEVEN STEPS TO BUILDING NEW HABITS

Having spent my adulthood in pursuit of a values-based life, I've gained a great deal of insight into the process of adopting new habits. Based on my experience, as well as research and conversations with others in this area, I've identified seven steps that can help you build new habits for your values-based life.

Step 1: You Know It's Harder Than You Think It Is

We know there's neuroscience behind why it's hard to change a habit. Yet even when we know something intellectually, that doesn't mean we'll actually believe it applies to us. That's the first step: to accept the fact that—no kidding around—this will be really hard, and probably harder than we imagine. That shouldn't discourage you; actually, it should do the opposite. By acknowledging the difficulty from the very beginning, you can keep yourself from becoming frustrated, disillusioned, and discouraged.

Unrealistic expectations that result in failure (like James, with his attempt to commit to an hour of self-reflection every day) can lead to negative thoughts of "why can't I do this?" and the defeated attitude of "I've failed so many times, why should I even try?"

Self-reflection can counter these negative thoughts, replacing them with positive affirmations. "I know that changing this habit is going to be hard. That has nothing to do with being good or worthy. I am a good person with a lot of good traits. I understand that building this new habit is a process, and I'm going to be accountable and get support along the way." With a positive attitude, you'll find it becomes much easier to start and sustain the hard work of changing a habit.

Step 2: Even Though It's Hard, You Really Want to Do This

Once you acknowledge how hard it's going to be to change a habit and adopt a new behavior, you ask yourself, "Do I really want to do this?" If so, then you need to be self-reflective about what it's going to take. For example, let's say that lifelong learning is one of your values. To put that value into action, you decide to take a class that will be both intellectually stimulating and life-enriching. This is going to be great, you tell yourself as you sign up for the class—and it will be, provided that you're realistic about the workload and the time commitment.

If a new habit or activity really is important to you, then what will you give up or do less of? It becomes a matter of prioritization (which is an ongoing process, as we discuss more in chapter 5). You might think it will be an easy trade-off: going back to graduate school and attending classes at night versus spending ten hours a week watching television. But when you've had a hard day at work, you're tired, and you really don't feel like studying, that television remote control is going to look like an old friend.

You don't have to be a tyrant when it comes to your time, but you must be realistic. By viewing everything in context of your life buckets and your 168, you'll avoid undermining yourself by not committing enough time to a new habit or activity. In the same way, you'll also become more discerning and avoid overcommitting to activities that just aren't enough of a priority right now. Although you want to do them one day, you just can't commit right now.

Let me share a personal example. When I was an undergraduate at Lawrence University, I fell in love with liberal arts. I started making a list of all the books I wanted to read during my lifetime. Back when I was 21 years old, I decided I was going to read every single book on my list. To start, I even bought four of them. Today, they're still on my bookshelf—unread.

About a year ago, I found summaries and reviews of the best books: *1,000 Books to Read before You Die: A Life-Changing List* and

1001 Books You Must Read before You Die. I bought both of these volumes, thinking this was going to be much easier. I could read summaries of the great books and become familiar with all of them. But when these two volumes arrived, I discovered that each is hundreds of pages long! It's been seven months (and counting), and I haven't opened them yet.

Am I discouraged? No, just honest with myself. As I review my 168 and examine my life buckets, I see activities and commitments that are very important to me: meaningful time with my family, teaching, working, trying to make a difference, doing volunteer work with the Archdiocese of Chicago, exercising regularly, writing this book, and more. Each activity represents a commitment that helps me live a values-based life. As I self-reflect, I can see that this is not the time to drop or reduce any of those other activities in order to read the 1,000 greatest books. At some point in my life when I reprioritize my activities, there may be more time for the great books. If and when that occurs, the great books will be waiting for me. For now, though, I am at peace with the fact that I'm making the best choices that work for my 168 and the life buckets I've defined for my values-based life.

Here's another example: during nearly 40 years of marriage and raising five children, my wife and I have taken countless pictures—at every holiday, vacation, get-together, birthday, anniversary, and graduation. All those pictures are currently in shoeboxes stored under our bed. Julie reminds me frequently that one of these days, I should organize those pictures. Julie is right, and I'm definitely going to do that. Just not now, because the time it would take to sort through all those pictures, put them in albums, and label them would require me to reallocate my 168. The pictures are treasured memories, but they just aren't a high enough priority right now. As I assure Julie, I will get to them one day. I tease her that I'll probably be in my eighties by then and may not remember who the people in the photos are. But I'll get to those photographs, one of these days.

Step 3: This Is What Works Best for You and Your Life Today

Sometimes when we want to make a change, we look around at what other people are doing and decide, "I should do that, too." Rather than select a goal that would work best for us, we decide that we'll just take someone else's prescription.

Let's say your doctor has suggested that you lose weight and start exercising to reduce your body mass index (BMI) and your risk of diabetes. It's a real wake-up call. As you consider what you can do to get in shape, you start paying more attention to your physically fit and healthy-looking neighbor who runs every day—even in the rain. You decide, "I should do that, too."

Now you haven't walked more than a few blocks for the past 20 years, but you're convinced that if running is good for your neighbor, it must be good for you. And if you're going to start running, why not commit to a marathon in a few months? So you buy a pair of running shoes and set out for your first run. After a quarter mile, you're winded, your knees and ankles ache, and you're miserable. You drag yourself back home, convinced that there's no way you can start exercising. Discouraged, you find solace in a carton of ice cream from the freezer.

To adopt new habits, you need to select goals and habits that are right for you. This is what makes goal selection so important, so that you're focused on changes that make the most sense for you and increase the likelihood of being successful.

My friend and colleague Fred Harburg, a clinical professor of executive education at Northwestern University's Kellogg School of Management, observed that the number one New Year's resolution is to lose 30 pounds. (This number is particularly significant, Fred said, because being overweight by 30 pounds or more is the definition of obesity.) But most people's experience of losing and regaining weight shows that this goal is not very effective. The reason, Fred explained, is that it focuses on the effect—weighing 30 pounds less—and not the cause, which is all about dietary and exercise habits.

"A better objective is to eat differently and to really define what that means. Then a person needs to engage in this behavior for a long enough period of time so that it becomes habitual," Fred said. "That way you're changing the cause, not the effect." The challenge, he added, is that we live in a results-driven world that demands instant change—as in our example of the person who thought he should be able to run a marathon in two months even though he'd never jogged before. Focusing on the cause can help us determine what will enable us to pursue the goal of being healthier, spending more meaningful time with friends and loved ones, or becoming a lifelong learner.

Habits are built slowly over time, starting with where you are. Maybe a better solution for someone starting out on an exercise regimen is to ride a stationary bike while watching television. As the fitness habit builds, the next steps may be to work with a trainer, see a nutritionist, join a gym, or take a fitness class with a friend to keep you both accountable. That's much more doable and sustainable for you than deciding you should be exactly like your neighbor, the running enthusiast.

The takeaway here is that whatever you select, make sure your new habit fits you, instead of just defaulting to someone else's choice.

Step 4: You Know It's Going to Take a Lot of Time and Practice to Get Better at Whatever You're Doing

You love music. You sing along with the radio as you're driving. When you were younger, you played guitar. You have fond memories of your grandmother playing the piano and leading the sing-alongs at family parties. Next time everyone gets together, you want to be the one playing the piano and singing.

You're committed, and you have allocated the time in your 168. What you didn't count on was just how hard learning the piano would be in the beginning and how bad you'd be at it. You thought some natural talent (thanks to your musical grandmother) was going to kick in and you'd be an instant musical prodigy. Instead, you're spending a lot more time than you expected on the basics, and practicing the C-major scale for a week isn't much fun.

Getting good at something is a process; that's how we learn and grow. If you accept that fact, then you won't get discouraged by false expectations of instant mastery. You have to practice with "Mary Had a Little Lamb" long before you can progress to Beethoven's "Moonlight Sonata." Virtually everyone is terrible at whatever they're trying to do for the first time, whether it's playing a musical instrument or gourmet cooking.

Without realistic expectations, though, you'll derail yourself. If you're not good at something right away, you may be tempted to think you are a failure and not keep trying.

Step 5: You're Building Incremental Goals along the Way

Knowing that it takes time to adopt a new habit and gain proficiency, don't wait until you've achieved mastery to acknowledge your progress. You need incremental goals along the way. Each milestone you achieve keeps you motivated. Let's say you've just gotten into running and you dream of completing a marathon one day. But right now, you're trying to run a mile without stopping. The first time you hit that milestone, celebrate! It doesn't matter how long it took—you completed your first mile. That feeling of accomplishment is not only a feel-good moment; it's also essential to sustaining a new habit by building expectations in your brain.

As Duhigg wrote in *The Power of Habit,* you need to start with a cue that triggers your new habit (he gives the example of putting on your running shoes before breakfast) and establish a reward for when you accomplish your goals. But the real staying power comes from anticipating that reward. "Only when your brain starts *expecting* the reward—craving the endorphins or sense of accomplishment—will it become automatic to lace up your jogging shoes each morning," Duhigg explained. "The cue, in addition to triggering a routine, must also trigger a craving for the reward to come."[2]

No matter how big or small the accomplishment, it's tangible progress. If you just managed to play "Happy Birthday" on the piano without hitting one wrong note, then stand up and take a bow. You don't have to be the next Mozart to feel that you've accomplished something. Each step you take is part of a lifelong journey of becoming your best self.

Step 6: You Find People to Support You and Hold You Accountable

When you're making a significant change—for example, quitting smoking after 20 years—it's hard to do it alone. Having someone to support you and hold you accountable can greatly increase your chances of success. Research into 12-step programs shows that those who engage with others are often twice as successful in maintaining abstinence as those who do not.

Support can take many forms, depending on the goal you set for yourself. It can be as simple as telling a good friend or your significant other that you are adopting a new behavior and asking them to hold you accountable. Being held accountable doesn't mean having a cheerleader who thinks everything you do is wonderful. What you need is someone who will hold your feet to the fire on making change—what Fred Harburg calls *real accountability*. "We have this infinite capacity for self-deception, so we need the perspective of others," he said. "This isn't surrounding ourselves with people who will stroke us and tell us what we want to hear. Genuine accountability means having people who will give us straight talk. That means real commitment with consequences. When you have that, the rate of success for making a change goes up 90 percent."

Mutual accountability can be established by partnering with someone who wants to adopt the same habit or lifestyle change. Sandy works in a restaurant I sometimes frequent. When I saw

Sandy recently, I complimented her on how healthy she looked. "I've lost 50 pounds," she told me proudly.

This wasn't her first attempt, Sandy explained, but it was her most successful because for the first time, she wasn't "dieting"—she was engaged in healthy eating and exercise as a lifestyle change. (As Fred Harburg described it, Sandy was focused on the cause, not the effect.) But the real secret to her success, Sandy told me, was that she, her husband, and her sister had all joined the same program, which included education, support, and measuring goals. "We're doing it together," Sandy said. "This way we can encourage each other and hold each other accountable."

Mutual accountability helps keep us on track and motivated. When one person loses focus or slips back into old habits, the other person is there to help them get back on track. It's a real partnership, not a competition, so that everyone can win.

I've seen this in business with groups that establish norms right from the start. They decide in advance how the people will behave in a group, especially how they interact with each other. There are clear expectations of what is and is not acceptable.

Let's say you're in a group of four people who get together weekly to discuss a project and report on the progress. The agreement is the four of you meet in person every Thursday at 3 p.m. Before the first meeting, your group discusses the expectations that everyone must be on time and present. Consequences are also set in advance: if someone is chronically late or fails to do his or her share of the work, that person is off the project. You and your group also decide how you'll interact with each other. Maybe someone is bothered by the use of four-letter words, so the group decides that foul language is not acceptable. The group may emphasize the importance of everyone being able to share their ideas and opinions freely, without fear of being shut down by others.

Now, as the project unfolds and the group gets together on a weekly basis, the norms and expectations will inform and guide each person's behavior. As an example, on your way to an in-person meeting, you pass a Starbucks and think how good a latte would taste right now. But there's a line, which means you'd show up five or ten minutes late. That's inconsistent with what the group has agreed to, so that latte will have to wait until after the meeting.

This model can be encapsulated in four parts:

1. Set clear expectations.
2. Communicate the expectations repeatedly.
3. Hold people accountable.
4. Establish consequences (both positive and negative).

What works in team projects also applies to our personal goals, especially in the context of being held accountable. You can adopt these four elements yourself: setting clear expectations for yourself, reinforcing those expectations in your self-talk and your daily self-reflection, holding yourself accountable, and establishing consequences if you succeed or fail in doing what you say you will do. For real accountability involving another person, these four components become a framework for making a mutual commitment and holding each other accountable. When everyone on the team is committed, the chances of success increase significantly.

I experienced mutual accountability when I was an undergrad. My roommate and I decided to take up running. In the beginning, it was easy and fun: we ran two or three miles together every morning before classes. Then there were those mornings when I thought, "I don't think so—not today." But I'd see my roommate putting on his shoes and I knew I had to get going. There were also days when he was tired but ran because I was heading out the door.

More than 40 years later, I'm still jogging several times a week. When I can, I run outside, but when the weather is bad or I'm traveling, there are no excuses: I get on a treadmill or elliptical. Over the years, running and exercise have become a regular habit—thanks to that mutual commitment made more than 40 years ago.

Step 7: You Measure Your Progress

What gets measured gets managed—and this applies to your personal goals and habits. You'll need to measure and track your progress. You can do this the old-school way of keeping a paper log. For example, I got into the habit about 20 years ago of weighing myself first thing every morning and recording my weight in a little notebook. When my weight goes up by ten pounds, I know I'm out of balance. Maybe I've been traveling and not exercising as much, or I've been on vacation with the family and enjoying a few too many hot fudge sundaes.

When I need to bring my eating habits back into balance, I have a chart with categories for soda, desserts, candy, and bread. At the end of every day, my goal is to have a zero in each of those categories. I'm very motivated to write down my zero—the feeling of satisfaction is a reward for me. So if I go to a meeting and there's a tray of cookies, I won't take one because I want to write down that zero. By measuring and recording, I bring myself back into balance.

Carter Cast, who self-disrupted his life by making dramatic changes (see chapter 3), uses a similar method to keep track of how well he lives his values week to week. He calls this system his *7–5–3–1*, which is a code for how he wants to live his life and allocate his time. It's complementary to your 168 and the life buckets into which you allocate your time. Here's how Carter explains the 7–5–3–1:

- **7:** Seven days a week, he spends with his "friends, the great thinkers." This involves reading for 20 to 90 minutes per day (depending on his schedule).
- **5:** Five days a week, he meditates for 20 minutes. Closing the door and the blinds in his office, he can create a space for meditation and clear his mind just before he goes off to teach a class.

- **3:** Three days a week, he gets his heart rate above 140 beats per minute for 30 minutes. "And I stretch now," he added with a smile. "The aging process."
- **1:** One day a week, he has a "meaningful conversation" with another person. Carter asks people he cares about or people he'd like to know better for a cup of coffee or lunch or dinner. "This is a codified way for me to stay connected to significant others and to learn from friends and associates," he said.

By tracking his progress on the 7–5–3–1, Carter can see where and when he falls short and how to reengage with his life plan. He's focused on accountability, not perfection. As I've stated before, and it's important to remind ourselves, we're all works in progress, which means we're never fully in balance. Be patient. Set reasonable goals that encourage you and track your progress.

There are many apps and tools that can help you, such as personal fitness devices that track everything from how many steps you take in a day to how much sleep you're getting each night. You can set alerts on your phone that remind you to get up and stretch or engage in mindfulness.

Discover what works best for you to measure your progress. You won't hit the mark every time, but by measuring your results, you'll increase your chances of being on target more often.

SELF-REFLECTION FROM START TO FINISH

Self-reflection starts you on the path toward building new habits by selecting the right goals that align with your life buckets and your 168. Along the way, self-reflection helps you be accountable. You see what's working—where and when you are making progress—and where you're facing obstacles and challenges. Maybe healthier eating is a real challenge on the weekends.

You do well Monday through Friday when you're busy, but with relaxation time comes an old habit of getting out the snacks. As we know by now, the cues and association between habits (watching a movie equals eating popcorn with extra butter) can undermine us if we aren't aware. But with self-reflection, we can identify what triggers lead us away from our new habit.

For example, I love chocolate and especially M&Ms. Left to my own devices, I'd devour them by the handful. With self-reflection and more mindfulness, I know I can enjoy one or two M&Ms to give myself a treat. When I'm more aware of what I'm doing, I'll make better choices.

As you build new habits and change the old ones, self-reflection is your constant companion. Ask yourself, "What does this new goal look like in my life? How will I know when I'm on track? What will I do when I'm out of balance? How will I keep motivated when my new habit becomes a challenge?"

This does not have to be a lot of work—one more thing on a to-do list that's already pretty long. Just be aware of your goals as part of your daily reflection on how you lived your life that day. Think about your new habit. "How did I do? What challenged me? Based on what I learned today, what will help me progress tomorrow?"

The more self-aware you become, the more information and insight you'll have into what works for you. Then it's only a matter of time before your new habit is well ingrained in your behavior and routine. As I stated in chapter 1, you'll always be a work in progress, but the rewards will be well worth the effort.

NEXT STEPS TO BETTER BALANCE

Building new habits takes time and patience. In order to make sustainable change, focus on one or two life buckets where you want or need to make changes. Doing too much all at once is a recipe for failure and disappointment. Focusing on one habit at a time will help you build the muscles you need to adopt new behaviors and start seeing change in your life.

- Identify one or two changes you want to make. Know *why* you want to make that change and how that relates to your values and your 168.
- Be very specific. Don't set a vague goal of "being healthier." Come up with specifics—for example, walk 20 minutes a day. When you're successful at that and begin to see results, you can expand to 30 minutes or longer. Don't go on a diet; set specific ways to eat healthier.
- Measure your progress. Day by day, write down when you successfully execute the changes. This isn't punitive—it's only between you and you. However, holding yourself accountable will help you see what's working and what isn't.
- Find your support system. Maybe you use a coach, which can be for physical fitness or career development. Maybe you join a group that meditates together once a week. Whatever your specific goals, find others who are on similar journeys. You can keep each other accountable and motivated.

CHAPTER 5

THE ART OF BEING PLANFUL—AND SPONTANEOUS

G iven all the things you're juggling—the push and pull from so many parts of your life—your 168 can overwhelm you. The only way to manage it is by being planful. Let me explain what I mean. My definition of being planful combines *planning* with *mindful.* It's an attitude and a habit that will increase your awareness of what you want and need to accomplish both now and over the longer term.

If we really drill down to the essence of being planful, we see that it's not realistic to just let life happen. Of course, you need to be flexible to manage the unexpected—both positive and negative. The planning part, however, still comes first.

This probably sounds simplistic, maybe even obvious—like saying that in order to live, you need to keep breathing. Your reaction might very well be, "Of course, I'm doing that!" But based on my observations and interactions with people, from students to senior executives, I can tell you that it's usually the opposite. For most people, life is one constant fire drill. They run from one thing to the next, creating confusion and chaos for themselves and everyone around them. This turmoil doesn't erupt only when there's suddenly a major problem to address or even a surprise call from an old friend who is in town. Their fire-drill mentality is the norm.

Although I have plenty of opinions about the importance of being planful, before sharing any of my thoughts on the subject, I wanted to research what the experts in personal growth and leadership have to say on the topic. Truthfully, there's not much. Shockingly, this topic gets little attention—not in Stephen Covey's *7 Habits of Highly Effective People* or any of the rest of business literature on becoming your best. What came closest was a blog that quoted an old Yiddish saying: *Mann tracht, und Gott lacht—Man plans and God laughs.* The message was that, even though we plan carefully, life is unpredictable. That's true—we all need to be flexible and adaptable. But what we're discussing here goes far deeper.

Living a values-based life, with time allocated to the life buckets that are most important to you, starts with awareness and deliberate planning—day-to-day and over the longer term. Otherwise your life journey isn't going to have a map. You'll find yourself speeding along at 90 miles an hour without a clear reason of where you're going and why.

By being planful, you know what your obligations and commitments are. You identify your top priorities. You'll know realistically how long it will take to complete a task and even how long it takes to get from place to place (it's shocking how people underestimate things like logistics). Don't mistake being planful as time management or keeping a calendar. As a combination of planning and mindfulness, being planful is the key to ensuring that you're living a values-based life with time allocated to the life buckets that matter most to you.

Equally important, if you are not planful, you will undermine all your good intentions for building those great new habits (as we discussed in chapter 4). The time you're trying to devote to meditating, exercising, biking to work, or whatever you want to do will be taken up by multiple distractions, unforeseen events, and things you forgot about.

How and where you can most easily reprioritize depends on your life circumstances. There is a big difference between operating by yourself and sharing your life with another person. Maybe you have a newborn, and what used to be a solid night's sleep from midnight to 6 a.m. has become a pattern of waking up every two hours. As your life changes, your job changes, and your family situation shifts, you'll have to change how you plan and prioritize. There will be periods of time when you have more complications and responsibilities, and then new and different ones.

Self-reflection to identify and stay true to your values is the foundation. You're always asking yourself what matters most and keeping track of how you are doing, for greater alignment across your values, choices, and actions. No one gets this perfect—we're always works in progress. Some days you'll be closer to the mark than others. However, having a plan leads to awareness, clarity, and calmness.

SPONTANEITY: THE BETTER HALF OF BEING PLANFUL

To be honest, right about here is where I usually lose a few people. Between the preamble on why I think planning is the key to a better life and the details of how to become more planful, there's usually pushback. Some people fall into MEGO mode—*my eyes glaze over*. In their minds, the fact that they have digital calendars and reminders on their smartphones means that they're planful. But there's a big difference between putting something on a calendar and managing your 168 in a planful way.

Others have a more visceral reaction. For example, when I recently gave a speech on living a values-based life, one woman in the audience spoke up. "Just listening to you, I feel like I'm in a straitjacket." Her attitude was "thanks, but no thanks" because being planful sounded to her like no fun without any chance for spontaneity. Until you actually treat your 168 like the precious resource that it is, it can feel a little constricting to plan and track your time, day by day. But it's actually the opposite. When people are not planful, they end up procrastinating and then rush to finish their work. Being planful is the only way I know to avoid going into freefall and losing all degrees of freedom every time your schedule changes. Being planful helps you prioritize—and reprioritize—everything you're facing on a daily basis.

Another payoff—and this surprises a lot of people who don't make the connection at first—is that being planful helps with and even encourages spontaneity. The secret is constant reprioritization as new issues arise that must be addressed immediately—and when there are opportunities for spontaneous fun. By being self-reflective and planful, you can handle whatever arises. The better you've managed your time, the more likely you'll be able to say yes to things you want to do in the moment—like that last-minute offer from a friend for tickets to a concert or a sporting event. But if you haven't planned and prioritized, and now you're up against a hard deadline on a work project, then you're stuck. Someone else is going to take those tickets.

Before going into the process of being planful, let's go deeper into the payoff (this will be especially appealing to the skeptics reading this). Here's a story I like to tell about my undergraduate days at Lawrence University. It was about eight o'clock on a Sunday evening and I was just about to sit down with some friends to play cards. In came my roommate, Brian, carrying about 12 books. He had a cigarette in his mouth (many people smoked in those days) and a panicked look in his eyes.

"What's with all the books?" I asked him, half-joking.

"History term paper," Brian told me. "It's due tomorrow."

I was taking the same class, so I knew which paper he meant—the final project that had been assigned four weeks ago.

"How much do you have done?" I asked him.

"None of it. I have twelve hours to do this."

While Brian settled in for an all-nighter to research and write a 20-page paper, I quietly headed out for the card game.

The difference? I had learned at an early age the benefits of being planful and the perils of procrastination. When I received the assignment four weeks earlier, I planned for it. I knew I didn't want to wait until the last minute, not only to avoid the stress but also in case something came up—whether another big assignment or a chance to have some fun. I planned when I would start and how much of the paper I needed to complete each day; as a result, I finished the paper several days ahead of the deadline. That's why I was playing cards while Brian was tearing his hair out and losing a lot of sleep.

Another story from my undergraduate days: I had a Friday afternoon show on the college radio station, WLFM. I called it "Give My Regards to Broadway"—and yes, I played show tunes. I can remember friends who definitely had different tastes in music (Led Zeppelin, Jimi Hendrix, The Doors . . .) commenting, "Did somebody just play 'The Music Man' on the air?" So maybe I didn't have that many fans. But I also was responsible for the six o'clock evening news broadcast. I'd rush into the station about five minutes before, tear off some stories from the teletype, and figure out what I was going to read on air.

It just so happened that the Chicago Cubs were playing the Cincinnati Reds (Pete Rose was playing in those days!) at Wrigley Field. As media interviews were being arranged, WLFM was invited to participate. Here's the kicker: this was right before midterm exams, and the sports director couldn't go because he had to study. This meant I had four media passes. I asked one friend after another to drive with me to Chicago and spend the afternoon at Wrigley Field interviewing the players. Person after person told me there was no way—he or she was cramming for exams and would be all night. But because I'd been planful, reviewing and studying all along, I could go—and I had a great time meeting all the Chicago Cubs and Cincinnati Reds players at the media event.

Planning sets the baseline, like mapping out a journey, whereas flexibility allows for the spontaneity. Every summer, my family takes a two-week road trip. By being planful, I can tell you when we're leaving and when we will be back home. I have a route mapped out with specific destinations, and I can tell you approximately how many miles we have to travel each day to stay on course.

This year we took our youngest son, Daniel, on a two-week trip to visit colleges from Chicago to Maine. We knew roughly where we wanted to be at any point along the trip. However, we were flexible and allowed for spontaneous changes in plans. When we were in Philadelphia and saw some old friends, we decided to stay a few extra days. This was all possible because we planned everything ahead of time, which allowed us to make adjustments in our schedule.

Knowing your priorities of what must get done also helps you plug into your fun bucket when you have an unexpected allocation of time. These are those precious moments to recharge your battery. When I was CEO of Baxter, I often had meetings every hour throughout the day. But when my assistant, Kathy, would tell me that my 3 p.m. meeting was cancelled because of flight delays, I knew exactly what to do. I grabbed my car keys, drove to a McDonald's nearby, got a Diet Coke at the drive-thru, and sat in the back of the parking lot with some Bruce Springsteen tunes cranked up full blast. Forty-five minutes later, I was back in the office, relaxed and refreshed.

Just recently, after a meeting finished early, I suddenly discovered a couple of free hours on my schedule. I reviewed my top priorities for the day and confirmed that I had addressed the key things that absolutely had to get done. I had already exercised that morning and my family was off doing their own activities. I decided to go to the movies (I must admit that for me, it really is about the popcorn with extra butter). It was exactly what I needed for my life balance.

Do you still think being planful is a burden? The truth is by not planning, you can end up squandering time. As pressures mount, you get locked in with few options and have to miss out on all the fun.

Assuming you're on board with being planful, let's take a look at how it works with a values-based life.

THE PLANFUL CONTINUUM

When it comes to being planful, most people fall somewhere along a continuum between completely avoiding it and fully embracing it. Here's how I define the stages along the continuum.

1. **No plan at all.** This is the extreme—the people who don't plan at all. It's as if they don't even know the meaning of the word.
2. **No time to plan.** Next are those who understand the concept of planning but tell themselves they have no time to think about it. They have confused activity and productivity, and they're in constant motion. They tell themselves that maybe when things slow down (which they never will), they'll think about planning.
3. **The partial planner.** These are the people who say, "I'm not only going to think about planning, I'm going to get a calendar and really organize myself." But they only put about one-third of the entries on the calendar. The rest is on scraps of paper or in text messages to themselves. Is it any wonder that they forget things and have conflicts they aren't even aware of?

4. **The myopic planner.** These people are diligent about planning. They really dig in, but only in one bucket: work. Pretty
   soon, they have all 168 hours scheduled with work to the
   exclusion of everything else, including sleep.
5. **The overwhelmed planner.** For these people, it starts off
   positively. They understand that it makes sense to be planful
   in all areas of their lives. But then they see just how much
   they have to do, and they get overwhelmed. There is no way
   they can fit it all into 168 hours—they need 250 hours a
   week for sure! So they stop planning.
6. **The planner who can't say no.** Further out on the continuum are the people who try to prioritize and put a great
   plan in place for themselves; however, they can't say no to
   anyone or anything. Day after day, the plan goes out the window, and they're always in a state of chaos and conflicting
   commitments.
7. **The planner who lets everyone plan for him or her.** Even
   with the best intentions of making a plan and prioritizing,
   these people get off track because they let everyone plan for
   them. If their boss "volunteers" them for a project, it may be
   hard to say no (although even then it's possible to be planful
   on when and how to work on it). Often, though, their significant other, friends, and family members are constantly
   making commitments for them. Better communication and
   boundaries are needed for sure.
8. **The prioritized planner.** These are people who plan with
   a realistic point of view. They acknowledge that they won't
   get everything done—it's just impossible. Instead, they prioritize, identifying the most important two or three items
   in each bucket. And when a higher-level priority emerges,
   they reprioritize.

If you're self-aware, you know where you are on the planning
continuum. As a work in progress, you may slide between one stage

and another. But the goal is to become a prioritized planner who is organized but not rigid. In fact, prioritization must be fluid and changing. You make plans but know they're not concrete. There will always be new priorities that pop up. In addition, you want to be spontaneous and able to shift your priorities—including to have some unexpected fun.

Here's how I practice being a prioritized planner. The night before, I review my plan for the next day. I know what my commitments and responsibilities are, as well as where I'm supposed to be and at what time (plus how long it will take me to get there). Based on this, I prioritize everything I want to do the next day. I even list my priorities in order, from highest urgency to lowest. I know approximately how long it will take to address my top priorities so I can be realistic about what I can expect to accomplish in a day. I don't just prioritize for work. My lists are a culmination of all my responsibilities and commitments, also including family, health/fitness, faith, fun, and making a difference.

The next morning, I start the day with a plan. But there will be phone messages and emails to respond to, maybe meetings I must attend at the last minute, and urgent matters to address. The list of priorities I made the night before may be completely reordered. Something urgent becomes the new top priority, and it takes half the day to address and resolve the issue. That leaves me with much less time to accomplish my other priorities (including what had been on the top of my list). Items that are further down on my list must be either postponed or eliminated. I will never be able to do everything. Constant reprioritization is the key.

FOCUSING ON WHAT'S MOST IMPORTANT

When we prioritize, we're not just labeling one project on our to-do list as being more important than another or identifying the most urgent problems that need our attention. It really is about life balance, which means we need to stay grounded in our values.

That's where daily self-reflection (as discussed in chapter 1) is crucial.

When things get really hectic—a major problem at work or someone close to us has a health crisis—our values become the guardrails for how we move forward. When we feel overwhelmed, we commit to doing the right thing and the best we can. Only with daily self-reflection do we even know what the right thing is.

The right thing is not one-size-fits-all. Just as each person's values will differ based on his circumstances and what matters most to him, so will his prioritization. Single parents who work outside the home need to be very clear in their minds (as well as with their bosses) that if the school calls and one of their children is sick, they must leave and spend the rest of the day working from home. It doesn't happen often, but when their children are running a fever or get hurt in sports practice, that's the far bigger priority than the in-person client meeting that was scheduled.

Restaurateurs who have invested everything—time, money, passion—into their restaurants know exactly what will happen if the chef is out on a night when every table is booked. The restaurateur will work an 18-hour day, because excellent customer service is a value and a top priority.

Although there may be some scrambling to cover the bases, there is comfort in being planful. At every point in time, you know what your priorities are. You know that things will change. But when you know your priorities, making time for them is a natural response. When people tell me that "I'd love to do x, but I don't have the time," it really isn't about the time. What they really mean (whether they know it or not) is that it's not a high-enough priority. It's okay to say no—in fact, you don't want to undermine your plan because you can't say no to someone.

Letting other people plan for you will get you off track. You've been traveling all week and want to relax, but when you arrive home, you find out that your in-laws are coming for the weekend.

Not what you had planned! This happened to me. I was in Dallas for a Christian leadership meeting in someone's home when I found out that the very same event was happening at *my house* the following Saturday with 40 or 50 people. I had already made plans that weekend for a reunion with college friends. When I spoke with Julie on the phone, she told me the calendar was empty, so she arranged the dinner at our house.

Even after nearly 40 years of marriage, plus teaching, writing, and speaking on the importance of being self-reflective and planful, I often don't get it right. (We're works in progress, remember?) There are two takeaways here. First, don't let other people plan for you and don't plan for other people. Now that my children are grown, I know I can't expect them to do things because I think it will be a good idea—they may have no interest.

Second, your planning affects others at home and at work. It's all about setting expectations, communicating effectively, being accountable, and having consequences. So if you agree to be planful and keep everyone informed, life will go far more smoothly.

Most important, by being self-reflective and staying true to my six buckets (as I listed in the introduction: work, family, faith, health/sleep, fun, and making a difference) and the relationship among them, I can be planful and pursue balance. If I really want to have flexibility, I know I must be planful enough to establish a base case—even though it will probably change. If I don't have a base case, however, I am not going to get as many things done as I would like and won't have time for spontaneity. That's why, whenever I reflect—for example, when I am on a plane—I go through my schedule, day by day, of what I am planning for the next six months.

For example, if I know that four weeks from now I will be in San Francisco, and someone wants me to give a talk there, I can tell them exactly what my plans are and combine it in one trip. As I've found, being planful and constantly reprioritizing enable me to be flexible, which helps with spontaneity. Life works more smoothly with less stress. And if that's not a reason to be planful, I don't know what is!

TRIAGE PRIORITIZATION

Everyone's job has its share of surprises. You think it's a routine day when suddenly your boss calls a meeting to announce a new initiative—and you've been chosen to lead it. A colleague has a family emergency, and you're covering his responsibilities for a week. At some point in your career, you're still going to face the unexpected.

Having spent the bulk of my career in the health care industry, I have so much respect for hospitals, clinics, and rehabilitation facilities. When I was CEO of Baxter, these institutions were more than just our customers; they really became our partners in delivering products that made a critical difference in people's lives.

Today, I am still close to the health care industry through Madison Dearborn Partners, where I serve on the boards of several health care companies. In addition, I've served on the board of directors of NorthShore University HealthSystem since 1997, including three years as chairman. Through this affiliation, I've gotten to known J. P. Gallagher, who is currently the president and CEO of NorthShore.

J. P. traces his long-term career plan in health care to growing up in a very supportive family with a clear sense of values that stayed with him throughout his life. Relationships were valued most—far more than anything material. These values were framed in a sense of faith with a connection to something much bigger, and with that came both a sense of relevance and obligation.

A defining time in J. P.'s life was between his senior year in college and his first year after graduation, when he lost three people who were very close to him. His roommate died in a small plane crash at the local airport, his brother-in-law committed suicide, and a close friend was shot during a carjacking. These tragic experiences instilled in him the desire to find a way to make a difference. This coincided with working at a health care consulting firm in Washington, DC. At the time, hospitals and health care providers were going through significant changes to improve quality and efficiency. By being self-reflective and in touch with his values, as J. P. headed off to graduate school, he set his sights on health care, where he believed he could make a difference in people's lives, especially during vulnerable times when they or their loved ones need care.

J. P.'s first job out of graduate school was with Advocate Health Care. He was enrolled in a training program at a Level 1 trauma center on Chicago's South Side. He recalled feeling "completely over my head" as he dealt with the complexity of day-to-day operations but had supportive bosses who allowed him to figure things out. "I remember being incredibly stressed—I was learning as I was doing," J. P. explained. "But I was also in the mix of something that really mattered. I was sprinting into what was right in front of me."

Although J. P. is not a clinician, he has spent most of his career running hospitals and hospital systems in which life-and-death decisions are made every day on the basis of prioritizing and reprioritizing patient needs. Any of us who has ever made a trip to a hospital emergency room has witnessed this firsthand: someone who is sick with a fever is going to be assigned a lower priority in the ER than someone who is bleeding and needs stitches. But if an ambulance rushes in a patient who is not breathing, that person now becomes the top priority and everyone else must wait to be treated.

In health care it's known as triage. Although many hospitals have made strides in reducing emergency department wait times, the practice of continually weighing priorities based on urgency is necessary to ensure quality health care delivery and positive patient outcomes.

"I'm a nonclinical person, so I'm not making those kinds of decisions. But I am working day to day with clinical staff who do make these decisions," J. P. said. "As a result, I appreciate the consequences of the decisions being made. As a leader, I have respect and admiration for what these people do to support patients. My job is to be supportive of them."

Outside of health care, prioritization does not typically involve decisions that affect people's health or, in the most extreme situations, literally have life-or-death consequences. But triage reminds us that prioritization is always relative. The designated number one priority now will move down the list if a higher priority emerges (whether a patient in the ER or a project that's just been assigned). If there's ever a doubt, reflecting on your values and what matters most can provide instant clarification.

WHEN PEOPLE MATTER MOST

The perspective that life really is short (as I like to say, "We're here for the blink of an eye.") leads most people to the realization that people do matter most. Although there can be urgent operational problems that take precedence, the people issues matter most.

"When you are triaging your day, the people stuff always comes first," J. P. said. That means when a human resource issue arises late on a Friday afternoon, he knows it can't wait until Monday morning. Or if he's deeply involved in strategic planning, but a member of his team needs to talk through a problem or challenge, the people issues need to be the priority.

As a leader, J. P. strives to demonstrate a "track record of valuing people." His three criteria for handling people issues are empathy, access, and clarity. Empathy compels him to look at the human side of every situation—even when a problem or situation demands accountability and punitive action. "When you seek to understand and convey some empathy or compassion for the person or situation, it allows you to move forward," J. P. reflected. "You're coming from a place of trying to do the right thing."

Accessibility for J. P. means being making himself available to others. For example, by walking the halls for 20 minutes a day, J. P. is not only more visible but also more accessible and approachable. "I want people to come up to me and say, 'There's an issue we need to discuss,'" he said. Moreover, this behavior sets a clear example for other leaders to increase their accessibility and visibility as a tangible way of putting a people-first set of values into action.

KEEPING LIFE FLUID

Reprioritization doesn't just happen on a daily or weekly basis as priorities shift and change. Our lives constantly shift and change. Young children who demanded much of our time become more independent as they grow up, then go off to college. Job responsibilities increase, making it harder to pursue as many pastimes and hobbies as we might like. But with retirement comes more time to pursue multiple interests. The ebb and flow of life both enables and requires us to be fluid in our plans.

A case in point is my friend Karen May, who assumed the chief human resources officer (CHRO) role at Baxter when I was the CEO. She went on to an impressive career at Kraft Foods and Mondelez International. She recently retired as executive vice president and CHRO of Mondelez and now serves on the boards of several companies. Although Karen was very planful in her life, these career moves were largely unexpected.

"When I was graduating from college, my goal was to become a partner in a public accounting firm. I thought I would marry the man I was dating, but I didn't see children as part of the picture," Karen said. "So what actually happened? I just retired as the CHRO of a $75 billion market cap company, and I have three children who are the loves of my life. My partner is who I thought it would be—my husband, Robert. But if you look at my life versus what I planned, I'm only one for three—so you might say I'm a complete failure. Or I am the luckiest woman on the planet as this unfolded."

Karen's story (which she shares in more detail in chapter 6) carries several lessons and takeaways—among them are taking a chance, asking for what you need, and giving things time to work out. The most applicable lesson for our discussion here is the importance of being fluid.

"Looking back at the start of my career, I don't think I should have had the goal of being a partner in a public accounting firm. That was too narrow. I would never recommend that for anyone I coach. It's better to have broad goals that help you set direction but allow for flexibility. Have a general plan, but don't box yourself in. My goal should have been to do cool, meaningful work on a team with talented people I respected and could learn from," Karen advised.

It's a matter of balance between having a desired general destination, while being flexible in how the journey unfolds. As Karen says, "You are being planful and flexible at the same time." As a working mother with a supportive spouse, Karen was able to pursue her life balance by integrating personal and professional goals, making it possible for her to take on new challenges while staying true to her values.

No one masters life balance. At times there are trade-offs—sometimes serious ones. If a problem is urgent, then everything else may need to be put on hold—whether spending time with your family, going to your children's sports games, or having a night out with your significant other. Instead of celebrating an occasion with friends, you may be on the next plane to handle a crisis in another country.

This is not about perfection, and there will be pressures from all sides. But self-reflection is the only way to stay true to yourself and accountable to your values. You may need to be all in on addressing a serious issue in one area of your life. But with self-reflection, you won't lose sight of those other priorities.

As you pursue balance, those other priorities move up on your list in support of living a values-based life according to your 168.

NEXT STEPS TO BETTER BALANCE

Review the eight stages on the planful continuum and reflect on where you are currently:

- No plan at all
- No time to plan
- The partial planner
- The myopic planner
- The overwhelmed planner
- The planner who can't say no
- The planner who lets everyone plan for him or her
- The prioritized planner

How can you use self-reflection to identify and stay focused on your top priorities? Remember, you'll never get everything done. But if you stay true to your plan and accomplish what is most important, you'll be in balance more often.

SECTION TWO

THE BALANCING
ACTION PLAN

CHAPTER 6

LIFE BALANCE IN REAL TIME

You have all the tools you need to manage your 168: self-reflection, avoiding surprises and the brick wall (and knowing what to do when you encounter them), building new habits, and becoming more planful. Now it's time to bring these tools together and in real time. This is where things get interesting and challenging.

It's like when you first learn a dance step. Going through the moves slowly, it doesn't seem that hard—left, right, left, turn. Then they put the music at tempo and you can't figure out where you are. That always happens to me when I take part in a Western line dance. As soon as the music starts, I'm the guy facing the wrong way, and there is an army of dancers marching toward me. (Julie has to come to my rescue, turning me in the right direction.) Or it's like when a football coach marks out a play with xs and os for where the players are supposed to move. But when the ball is snapped, suddenly what looked so simple on the coach's diagram becomes very real—and four huge defensive linemen are ready to mow you down.

And so it is with life balance. You're trying to become more planful, but new priorities keep popping up—as well as many distractions. You are trying to build new habits, but that takes so much energy when you're overwhelmed. Welcome to life!

In this chapter, we're going to go deeper into life balance in real time, amid all the pressures and unexpected things that can potentially derail us if we're not self-reflective and self-aware. Life balance doesn't just happen; it requires the ability and willingness to be flexible and adaptable. However, the payoff is being more in control of your life and enjoying those things that are most important to you.

KEEPING YOURSELF ON TRACK

Everywhere I go, whether I am talking to students, executives, academics, religious leaders, or any other group, I hear people express the desire for greater life balance. And I hear the same complaints: "I'm having trouble balancing my life." Maybe they are working full-time and going to school. Or perhaps they're single parents with small children, or they have a sick relative in the hospital. So many people are overwhelmed by mounting responsibilities. The only way to manage all these pressures is by practicing self-reflection. By continuously reflecting on our priorities and what matters most, we keep ourselves on track and course-correct toward better life balance.

At the same time, you need to recognize that often you will be out of balance. One area or another is going to consume far more time and effort than all the others. You could be in the middle of a significant work project; for example, your company is making an acquisition and you are part of the team that's working seven days a week for six weeks. Conversely, you or a loved one is facing a health crisis, and suddenly that becomes the top priority. Or maybe you're training for your first marathon; in the four weeks leading up to it, you're not at work as much as you usually are.

Life ebbs and flows; that's normal and natural. We don't want to be robotic about it. But over time—usually measured in weeks or sometimes months—you can pursue better balance by allocating your time to what matters most to you. Yet most people don't see it that way when they're in the thick of it. For example, among my MBA students who are going to school and working full-time, there are those who decide that life balance can wait. They tell me, "I am graduating soon, and then my life will get simpler." That might sound good in theory, but I've never seen that happen in real life.

As time goes on, life usually gets more complicated—not less. Let's say an MBA student is single and 28 years old when she starts the program. She's in a long-term committed relationship, gets married, and maybe has children. Her job is five times more complex than when she started working, with broader responsibilities and international travel. It's simply not realistic to assume that somehow life is going to slow down. You're on an express train, and the pace is only going to get faster. Admitting that reality is the first step in pursuing life balance.

Equally important is being able to recognize when you're out of balance. For most of us, imbalance starts gradually, then escalates. You skip your exercise routine one day and then a second day; before you realize it, a week has gone by and you haven't exercised at all. Or you stay up very late, working well past midnight to meet a deadline, telling yourself that one night of lost sleep won't hurt. Then the pattern repeats night after night, until you're living on caffeine and running on fumes. You reschedule plans with family or friends, saying, "We'll make it up soon." Now it's three weeks later, and there never seems to be enough time to keep that commitment.

Along the way, there will be signs when life is out of balance. Often those signs involve our emotions. We get triggered; we feel overwhelmed or angry. We lose our temper more easily. We catastrophize, imagining the worst possible outcome. We tell ourselves we're just stressed. Then someone makes a small comment, and we fall apart—or blow up. Sound familiar?

Here's how it sometimes happens in my life: I start out with a long to-do list and three top priorities I am absolutely committed to doing. I know what needs to be accomplished—first, second, third. Then, all of a sudden, I have five more things to do. Usually, I am very planful and good at prioritizing. I can look at the eight things on my plate and decide what must get done immediately and what can (or must) wait. But I confess there are times when I get overwhelmed. When that happens, everything feels like a top priority, especially if some things have to be done at the same time. I need to finish a project, I have a board of directors' call in a half hour, and one of my children needs to be picked up at the airport.

I'm the type of person (and there are a lot of us like this) who hates to let other people down. When I say I'm going to do something, I'm going to do it no matter what. My automatic response is usually to tell myself that I just have to go faster. Suddenly, I'm racing all over the place and becoming even more overwhelmed. Thankfully, Julie is there to step in at times like these. She tells me, "Slow down a minute. Maybe someone could help you." (Sometimes, she has to say it more than once.) Then she suggests that one of our older children can go to the airport, and she can run an errand that I had promised to take care of. Now, my to-do list is more manageable, and I can see my priorities more clearly.

There are two takeaways from this story. First, know the warning signs that you're out of balance. When you feel panicked, do you get short-tempered? Do you become a deer in the headlights not knowing what to do? With greater self-awareness of those advance warnings that you're out of balance, you can intervene with yourself. Sometimes it just takes five minutes of self-reflection. "What's going on that has me so worked up? What conflicts am I facing? Of all the things vying for my attention, what is really most important? If everything seems important, then what's the most critical? What is non-negotiable for me?" By slowing yourself down, you'll see and think more clearly.

Second, when life gets completely out of balance—whether for a day or over a longer period of time—you need someone in your corner to help you. It may be your spouse/partner, a close friend, a coach, or a mentor. This person knows you well enough to recognize when you're out of balance and is willing to tell you to take a time out. I've been fortunate in 40 years of marriage that Julie is this person for me, as I am for her. She recognizes when I am taking on too much or I am not devoting as much time to some of my life buckets because I'm overly concentrated in one area.

Even a short check-in with a confidante can help get you back on the right track. I was reminded of this when reading an October 2019 *Wall Street Journal* article titled "When These Executives Want Candid Advice, They Text," which described women executives who form ad hoc "text board of directors" to ask questions, seek advice, share ideas, and give answers. As the *Journal* noted, "What makes these text-based exchanges significant, proponents say, is that more professional women are gravitating to them to swap information immediately in a medium that encourages brevity, honesty, and a certain degree of vulnerability."[1] The same text board, I believe, could be useful for anyone needing a quick check-in or some instant advice on prioritizing.

TAKING A LOOK AT YOURSELF

Self-reflection does involve asking yourself a very probing question: is the way you're living your life aligned with what you say is most important? This is a moment of truth when you are accountable to yourself for living a values-based life.

There are times when we take a step back and see just how out of balance we are. Thankfully, nothing bad or permanently damaging resulted. We just have to laugh at ourselves. I find this to be extremely healthy. We shouldn't take ourselves so seriously—we are works in progress. And the humor makes it easier to see how and where we've let things get out of hand.

I travel a lot—several times a month for several days at a time. To keep myself organized, when I park my car at the airport, I always write the location of the parking space on my ticket, which I tuck away in my wallet. It's a routine that I follow every time.

One night, after flying home from Los Angeles, I couldn't find the parking ticket anywhere. I started to worry, but I remembered distinctly parking my car on the third floor. I walked that entire floor of the parking garage at O'Hare Airport—row after row of hundreds of parked cars. I couldn't find mine anywhere.

I was supposed to meet Julie for a late dinner in downtown Chicago, and I knew I was going to be late because I couldn't find my car. When I finally gave up looking and called Julie from my cell phone, she said calmly, "Harry, I have your car. When you left for Los Angeles the other day, you took a cab to the airport." (No wonder I couldn't find the parking ticket.)

We had a little laugh about it. Later that night, as I engaged in self-reflection, I began to ask myself how I had become so out of balance. Clearly the amount of traveling I was doing at the time contributed to it. I also saw that I had become so overwhelmed that I was on autopilot. Thankfully, a "missing" car that wasn't really missing was the only result.

Awareness is half the battle. If we don't catch ourselves when we are out of balance, we're in danger of thinking that imbalance is normal or to be expected. You may be in a job where occasionally you have to work 80 or 100 hours in a week. But if that continues for a longer period of time and it becomes a problem for you, it needs to be addressed before you're surprised (see chapter 2) or you hit the wall (see chapter 3). This is life balance in real time, using self-reflection to see where and how you are neglecting parts of your life and what you can do about it.

Everyone is different. Some people have three life buckets; others may have ten. Most people, I've noticed, have six in categories such as work (career/education), community/family, spirituality and mindfulness, health, fun, and making a difference. Your life buckets (see the introduction) reflect what is most important to you at a particular time. Work may be the biggest bucket at one point in your life and family in another. Leisure may be greatly reduced during certain periods and then take on more importance as you have more time, such as in retirement. There's no prescription or judgment here, only the advice to be mindful about how you allocate your time and energy to your buckets so that your 168 reflects your version of a values-based life.

Let's say you're an avid runner but your work and travel schedule prevent you from running for a week. There will be a point at which you say to yourself, "I have to run!" If you don't put yourself in motion soon, you're going to be miserable. You may feel the same way about yoga, playing music, writing in your journal, creating art, or any other activity that nourishes you. These are important outlets that make your life meaningful and reflect your values. Although you may have to put some things on hold from time to time, if it happens too frequently, you will be way out of balance.

SETTING BOUNDARIES AND SAYING NO

Sometimes getting your life back into balance comes down to one word: *no*. It's not a comfortable word for those of us who have busy lives, have multiple commitments, and don't like to disappoint people. However, there are times when the only way to bring ourselves closer to balance is by saying no. I had one of those moments just recently.

It had been a very long day that started with a meeting at seven in the morning, followed by a speech at ten, and then meetings all afternoon. Now it was evening, and I was driving in rush hour traffic to attend a black-tie dinner in downtown Chicago. To be perfectly candid, it wasn't an event that was important to me or that I was particularly looking forward to. It was one of numerous invitations that I receive. As I was driving, I asked myself, "Why am I going? There will be 300 people at this event. Will anyone notice—or care—if I'm not there?"

The answer was no. And with that, I got off the highway at the next exit and turned around. I went to the gym, exercised for an hour, and then took a late-evening walk with Julie. Balance was restored in the moment. Understand that I'm not advocating breaking commitments, but it's easy to get so caught up in what you think you should do without really thinking through whether it makes any sense. You may be on autopilot without even noticing it.

Unnecessary pressure and unrealistic expectations can affect all aspects of our lives, especially work. If we don't set reasonable expectations for what we can do, we allow ourselves to become overwhelmed and out of balance. The more self-aware we are, the sooner we can catch ourselves before we're significantly off the rails.

An example of someone who uses self-awareness to balance her life is Anna Budnik. I've known her for many years; she was an MBA student in my values-based leadership class years ago, and I have given several talks at her company. Today, Anna is a senior executive for Willis Towers Watson, where she heads Retirement for the Global Services & Solutions Practice Area. Thinking back on her career, Anna reflected that one of the things she had to learn was that not everything had to be done right now. "When I was younger and just starting out, I was always worried about getting in trouble if I couldn't do something or had to reschedule," she said.

That led to many late nights in the office—even staying there overnight—and going in on weekends. Fortunately, her manager pulled her aside and explained that not everything was a crisis. "My manager told me, 'Not everything is a priority—we're not brain surgeons.' That had an impact that lasted throughout my life, allowing me to prioritize and to know that it's okay to ask a client for a little more time."

With experience came a better sense of her priorities, Anna explained. A simple example is her email, which may at times include as many as one thousand unread messages. "But I know which ones I can skip and the ones I need to respond to immediately. I keep the unread messages until I have to get to them," she said.

The bottom line, she said, is ensuring that you're communicating with people inside and outside the firm, making sure that people have the information they need and a clear understanding of the deliverables. "At the end of the day, if you have the reputation for delivering, it allows you to prioritize. That's what I wished someone told me earlier when I started my career. That would have been a valuable perspective," she said.

WHEN YOUR LIFE PLAN CHANGES

Over the long term, your life will change, personally and professionally. For many of us, life gets more complicated because there are more moving parts. Our priorities and commitments change, as do our interests and how we want to spend our time. In addition, opportunities arise that take us in new directions.

Along the way, our life balance changes. To manage these changes, we need to be self-reflective. Most important, in my experience, is being willing to be open and flexible, which enables us to become more balanced.

My friend Karen May, whose story I shared briefly in chapter 5, is one of the best examples I know of someone who has been adaptable as her life changed, while pursuing balance in areas that are the most important to her, including career, family life, health, and leisure. For example, early in her career, while Karen was a CPA with a major accounting firm, her husband, Robert, announced that he had a great job offer—in New York. But Karen's job was in Chicago—the city they had agreed, as a couple, to live and work in. But being flexible, and with Robert's encouragement, Karen approached her boss with the possibility of a transfer. "Within five minutes they said yes," Karen recalled. The result is what Karen calls an important lesson: *if you don't ask, you will never know.*

At that juncture in her life, Karen's career bucket took precedence as she pursued the goal of becoming a partner in a public accounting firm. With open communication about their mutual life goals, Karen and Robert were partners to help each other advance.

Their life kept evolving, and with each major change, there was a shift in what Karen saw as most important. She and Robert were both back in Chicago when Karen decided she did want to have children. (Earlier, as related in chapter 5, that had not been part of her plan.) After returning to work following the birth of her first child, Karen was the only woman at her level at the firm trying to balance parenthood and a career on the partner track.

She asked for a little bit of flexibility. Her plan was to manage her biggest client, Baxter, which accounted for about 95 percent of her time. The other 5 percent, she requested, was for "flexibility as a new working mom." Even though Karen was essentially working full-time and had more billable hours than some full-time colleagues, the firm considered her a part-time employee.

"For the first time, I felt like I didn't belong there." Her next decision was to look for new opportunities, which she found within Baxter. Working three days a week (but the equivalent of nearly 40 hours), Karen worked a reduced schedule for the next several years, including job-sharing a VP-level role with another working mother. This arrangement, which was very unusual at the time, gave her the flexibility she needed to balance her life as a working mother while still building her career. That was another important life lesson, crucial for pursuing and maintaining life balance: *plant yourself where you thrive and feel that you can be yourself.*

"I didn't sleep a lot during that time in my life, but I learned to juggle my roles of a mom, a wife, a daughter, and still have a meaningful career," Karen recalled.

To put Karen's story in perspective, it's interesting to look at the research about women who pursue both high-powered careers and family life—particularly what was true for women when Karen was active in her career. Sylvia Ann Hewlett, an economist and expert in gender and workplace issues, published research findings in *Harvard Business Review* in 2002 that delivered a sobering reality at the time. "When it comes to having a high-powered career and a family, the painful truth is that women in the United States don't 'have it all.' At midlife, in fact, at least a third of the country's high-achieving women—a category that includes high wage earners across a variety of professions—do not have children." In addition, Hewlett found that women who were raising children suffered "insurmountable career setbacks." The data painted a bleak picture: "for too many women, the demands of ambitious careers, the asymmetries of male-female relationships, and the difficulties of conceiving later in life undermine the possibility of combining high-level work with family."[2]

In today's work environment, corporate policies and technology enable more flexibility in where, when, and how work gets done, which has resulted in some improvement in how both women and men balance home and careers. Nonetheless, we still have a long way to go.

After Karen had been with Baxter for several years, I asked her to consider working in human resources. It was a department she knew little about, as she kept reminding me. But I had faith in Karen's abilities, her proven track record in building and managing relationships, and her knowledge of what it took to be successful.

That night, she told Robert about the opportunity to go into HR. "I explained that, with Harry as CEO, instead of going 'warp one' speed, we'd be going 'warp ten' speed." Karen knew that meant working full-time—with a six-year-old, a three-year-old, and a newborn. Robert surprised her with a plan of his own. He had been contemplating taking a break from his job, so he encouraged her to go full-time while he became the stay-at-home parent. That willingness, on both their parts, to be flexible opened up more possibilities for them across multiple aspects of their lives.

"You have to give things a try to see if they will work for you and your family. What works for you may be different than what works for your neighbor," Karen advised. "Whether you're taking on a new job or work arrangement or hiring a new babysitter, try it for a month or so, and see how it feels. After a few months, check in on how things are working—not just what you think about things, but also how it feels in your heart and gut. Then make the necessary adjustments."

A key element to pursuing balance is understanding where you are trying to go, whether as a person, a couple, a unit, or a family. Karen and Robert have a common understanding of what they are trying to create together—the kind of home environment they want, their values, what they wanted to teach their children, and financial security. It wasn't a "you do this, and I do that" type of relationship, as Karen described it. Rather, it involved the "right constellation of decisions" that helped them achieve their goals.

THE HORIZONTAL LIFE PLAN

One way that people undermine themselves in their pursuit of life balance is to look at their goals separately, not as part of the greater whole of their 168. I've seen this among men and women, students and executives alike. They seem to look at each life bucket as if it's the only priority they have. (We see this in myopic planners in chapter 5, who go deep into one area and ignore the rest.) This is guaranteed to backfire because the goals (multiple and usually quite ambitious) that they set for themselves in each area are very difficult, if not impossible, to pursue in isolation.

Karen uses a simple framework with three columns (in conversation with her daughter and future son-in-law, Karen drew it on the back of a napkin over lunch). One column is for personal goals, one for professional goals, and one for financial goals. "So many people work on one column at a time, working vertically and deeply into each category. But you have to work horizontally, because a goal in one column influences the others," Karen explained.

She gave a hypothetical example of someone who wants to work two days a week, become a CEO, and be a millionaire. "That's probably not going to work," she said with a laugh. "Some people have trouble knitting their goals together. But when you work horizontally, it forces the trade-offs and helps you get deep alignment across all parts of your life."

Over the years, there were things Karen didn't want to give up but had to do less frequently. She couldn't garden like she wanted to, and she wasn't available to walk with a group of her friends every Saturday—only once a month. But in the context of the bigger picture, Karen had peace of mind and a sense of balance that she was making the best choices she could for herself and her family across the three columns of personal, professional, and financial goals. "Make thoughtful and conscious choices about what you're doing—and not doing. That helped me feel in control of my life balance. Those choices will, and should, ebb and flow over time as your work and family situation changes."

BUILDING TRUST AND TRANSPARENCY

Trust is a cornerstone in life balance, particularly in allowing yourself to be successful at work and present for what matters in your personal life. It starts with self-reflection and learning to trust yourself. Trust is built as you prove to your boss and colleagues that you can be counted on to get the work done. In many situations, it doesn't matter when or how long you work, provided that you meet the deadlines. That encourages better life balance, in jug-gling everything from client meetings and projects to soccer games and school plays.

At the same time, trust between you and your boss gives you the confidence to speak up and say what's going on in your life that requires more flexibility. It may be a significant personal event in your family (a graduation, a wedding), or it may be a sudden shift in family priorities because of an illness. With mutual trust, you can speak openly and bring your whole self into the conversation.

During Karen's career, she was open with her team about her schedule, personally and professionally. This helped others on her team do the same. As she saw it, it built trust and fostered greater transparency. When someone needed more flexibility, others stepped up to help, knowing that one day, they would probably need the same support and assistance.

When I was CEO of Baxter, I always encouraged my team to take the time they needed when they needed it—and it wasn't because I was trying to be a nice guy. I also wanted to make sure the work got done. I knew that when people were given flexibility, they were more likely to be incredibly loyal. There was another reason as well: striving for life balance has brought me great satisfaction, personally and professionally. As I look back on my leadership roles at Baxter, I am grateful I had the opportunity to be a role model for life balance.

I can remember being in meetings at five o'clock, and no mat-ter how important the discussion was, I had to tell people I was leaving because I had to coach 20 first-grade girls who were wait-ing for me at the local baseball field. I tried to set an example that balance was important; as a result, many people wanted to work on my team. Even though we pursued balance, we still worked hard to get the job done.

Where there is transparency, trust is strengthened even further. People can move beyond the fear about "what are they going to think?" in order to ask for what they need. Unfortunately, people can get locked into their fear and don't give themselves any chance of finding a flexible solution. For example, I knew a guy who, when his wife broke her arm, was too afraid of what his boss would think to tell him what was going on at home. When his boss asked him on very short notice to fly to New York for a meeting, the guy agreed, even though his wife was home alone with three young children, trying to manage with a broken arm. Could he have gotten out of the meeting? Could someone else have gone in his place, or could he have called in from home? Very possibly, but fear of saying something to his boss paralyzed him from exploring other possibilities. Had he been open and transparent with his boss all along, speaking up about a family emergency would not have been an issue.

LIFE BALANCE AND PERSPECTIVE

Now retired from working full-time and with her children on their own, Karen is building a new life balance. Although she serves on public company and nonprofit boards, Karen has more time to pursue gardening and other leisure activities. Karen looks back on her life with satisfaction, but also with a realistic view that not everything was perfect. She recalled some great advice she received from a pediatrician many years ago who told her, "You will not be great at everything every day. If you ask yourself every day, 'Was I a great mother? A great spouse? A great worker?' you will drive yourself crazy."

Instead, she did the best she could while relying on others—her husband, Robert, and her colleagues at work—to help manage what was most important to her. As Karen reflected, "People have the tendency to be very critical of themselves and think they have to do everything perfectly. If they are not 100 percent in everything, they feel like a failure. Because of this, you need to watch your self-talk and set your standards against your unique 168. Give yourself the grace to be confident in what works for you.

Your definition of success should be based on what works for you and measured against your goals, not someone else's." Through self-reflection, Karen learned how to trust herself to do the right thing and to do the best she could.

When pursuing life balance in the moment, day to day, or over the long term, this is wise advice. You can't live anyone else's life any more than you can be true to someone else's values that are not your own. You need to know your values, set your standards, and live the values-based life that matches what is most important to you. It will not be perfect or easy. At times it will be messy and frustrating. But even in the most challenging moments, it can be rewarding and lead to great satisfaction.

NEXT STEPS TO BETTER BALANCE

To help you manage your life balance, try Karen May's life goals framework. Write three column headings across the top of a piece of paper:

Personal Goals	Professional Goals	Financial Goals

As you write down your goals under each heading, work horizontally—not vertically. This exercise will help you see how your goals align. Engaging in goal setting in this way will help you keep a realistic view of what is possible, while acknowledging the trade-offs that are necessary to live your unique values-based life.

CHAPTER 7

STRENGTHENING FAMILY, FRIENDS, AND COMMUNITY

For many of us, family is one of the most important life buckets—if not the most important. Family is usually defined by having a spouse and children, as well as an extended family of siblings, parents, and other relatives. For others, family also includes people who are so close to them, the word *friend* just doesn't suffice. Our personal lives are further enriched by having enduring friendships and a sense of community. These people and connections give meaning to our lives, providing us a center. In this chapter, we'll approach family, friends, and community like concentric circles, one encircling the other. At the core is family, as you can see in figure 7.1.

MY FAMILY LIFE

For me, no matter how much time and attention I devote to other areas, family is the center of my life. It's been that way from as far back as I can remember. My parents and grandparents were my first and most important teachers; they taught me values such

Figure 7.1   *For many of us, our personal relationships are defined by family, friends, and community, which are concentric circles—with family at the core.*

as the importance of faith, respecting everyone, doing the right thing, and always doing my best.

One of my most vivid childhood memories was getting all As on my first-grade report card. My dad was so excited and proud. "I have to show this to your grandmother," he told me. I can still picture my grandmother reading each of my grades aloud and asking me questions about what I learned in school. This ingrained in me from a very young age the importance of doing well, because I wanted to make my family proud. When I got a little older, some of the other students would brag about not doing their homework. Whenever I thought about my dad and how proud he was to show my grandmother my report card, I *knew* I was going to do my homework. Even if he and my mother didn't tell me to do it, I didn't want to disappoint them.

My four siblings—Steve, Paul, Marilyn, and Tom—and I grew up knowing that Mom and Dad cared deeply about what was happening in our lives. At dinner, Dad would go around the table and ask each of us about our day; he genuinely wanted to know. Our parents were deeply involved in our lives, whether going to Little League games, going to the movies, or taking us to church every Sunday—not just dropping us off at the door to come back in an hour. They lived their values. In turn, their beliefs, attitudes, and actions shaped my thinking about my 168 and continue to keep me grounded.

Our parents also instilled in us the importance of loving each other. When my brothers and I were young and got into a fight, Dad would seldom yell at us. Instead, he would sit us down and start to cry (which was far worse than getting yelled at). He'd tell us how he did not get along with his brother and sister when he was young, which he deeply regretted. "No matter what, I want you all to get along," Dad would say as tears rolled down his face.

To this day, my brothers, my sister, and I call each other every few days. No matter how busy we are, we always make it a priority to get together at least twice a year. As I was writing this chapter, we had just returned from spending a weekend together in New York City. In addition, every few years, all 24 of us get together: my siblings and I, our spouses, and a grand total of 14 children. It's a real family reunion of laughing, reminiscing, and deepening connections. Equally important, it's a gift we give to the next generation in hopes that they, too, will carry on the closeness we've enjoyed throughout our lives.

When I met Julie Jansen in college—I was a senior and she was a freshman—one of the most important things we had in common was strong family ties. She was close to her parents and her six siblings. As we got to know each other, it was clear that we held similar values, deep religious faith, and a shared sense of purpose. How blessed we were to have met in college. We knew from a young age that we wanted to spend the rest of our lives together. It wasn't just an attraction—we were deeply aligned on what was most important to each of us. Before we got married, Julie and I discussed our beliefs and values, including how we intended to raise our children one day.

A STRONG FAMILY TO SUPPORT BALANCE

Being blessed with a strong family has helped me pursue balance. I'm surrounded by people who genuinely care about me. With them, I never had to worry about whether I got promoted or not, or how much money I made or didn't make. In fact, whenever I got promoted, one of their first questions was always whether I was taking care of myself or working too hard. For example, when I was named to a director-level position at Baxter, my mother asked me, "Are you getting enough sleep and exercise? Are you spending enough time with Julie and the children?" When I became chief financial officer, Julie told me how proud she was of me, but in the next breath she asked, "Are you still going to be Harry, or are you going to get caught up in the corporate mumbo-jumbo?"

From personal experience, I can tell you that a strong family will keep you grounded. When you're leading a big project and constantly working, your loved ones will intervene. You may even get asked some tough questions. "Are you going to keep working 80 hours a week, or are you going to start spending more time with the people who are most important to you?"

When someone you love says, "I don't have enough time with you. I need you to be here," then you have to face the reality of your 168. Chances are, you're severely out of balance. If you want to avoid surprises (see chapter 2) and prevent yourself from hitting the wall (see chapter 3), you need to invest time and effort in building a strong family. The people closest to you, with whom you share strong bonds, cannot become just one more thing on your to-do list. They form the center that keeps you from spinning out of control. Their presence in your life enhances your purpose and meaning.

THE FAMILY CHALLENGE

Having a strong family is a real positive—truly a blessing. However, given the reality of most people's lives, work and family can feel like two opposing forces. People who are building their careers and starting a family often feel that challenge day to day, from the logistics of who goes where to handling a long to-do list of what must get done. Most working parents (and I'm one of them) feel the push and pull of work and family.

Sound like pressure? It is—and this is the other side of having a strong family. You want to be home for dinner, to take walks with your spouse, and to help your children with their homework and coach their sports teams. Your time, however, isn't unlimited. You only have your 168. You can't be everywhere—not at every school event, soccer game, or activity. You have to make choices. This is hard, especially because each choice involves people you love and don't want to disappoint.

The only way to handle these difficult choices is by using self-reflection to help you stay focused on your values. You are committed to doing the right thing and the best you can do. However, the reality is you can't spend 100 percent of your time with your family. I can remember when Suzie, our oldest child, was in first grade and liked to talk to me when she got home from school. Julie would dial the phone number for her, and invariably the first question would be why I wasn't home. Her school was done at three o'clock, so why wasn't my work done?

Add to that business travel, late meetings, and board dinners—along with job demands that exceed a 40-hour week. As we've discussed (especially in chapter 6 on managing life balance in real time), it takes some juggling (along with planning and prioritization, as outlined in chapter 5). Some of those choices will mean spending more time working or focused on another life bucket, such as health (maybe you're training for a marathon) or fun (you play a sport regularly). No one can decide it for you. On some days, work will be the main focus; on others, it will be all about family. Sometimes, it will be a mix of both.

Without self-reflection, choosing what to do will be extremely difficult. Most likely, you'll be ruled by your emotions, especially guilt. There's nothing worse than being in one place—whether that is a work event or your third cousin's birthday party—and knowing you should be someplace else. With self-reflection, you can gain peace of mind and minimize the second-guessing of what you should have, could have, or would have done if you had a chance to do it over again (which, of course, you won't have). It's never going to be perfect and probably will be messy, but that's the reality of life and making choices.

BALANCING THE FAMILY BUCKET

The more self-reflective and self-aware you become, the more clarity you'll have. You'll make decisions based on your life circumstances, your commitments and prioritization, and your 168. You'll also get creative. For example, when my son Andrew asked if I could coach his Little League team, I knew there was no way I could be the only coach, but I didn't want to disappoint him. My solution was to reach out to three other dads with children on the team and the four of us agreed to share the coaching duties. We took a blood oath that at least one of us would always be at the game—and it worked.

By planning ahead and figuring out some things I could do on the phone or on the laptop, with a little flexibility I could make things happen. For example, in our neighborhood we had a Y-Guide program for first to third graders, including weekend camping trips, but with one condition: a parent had to go. Despite being busy, because I have five children each born about three years apart, I ended up in Y-Guides for 15 consecutive years. When it was lights out for the first graders at nine o'clock at night, I would sit outside the cabin with my laptop and internet connection device so I could do email in the woods.

I also found ways to combine some extra family time with work-related social events. For example, when I was in a corporate role, bankers or advisors would sometimes invite me to a Chicago Cubs game. I didn't want to spend a night away from the family, so I'd suggest an idea: they brought their children to the game and I brought mine. The children had a good time together, and the bankers and I had some time to talk business. (And Julie enjoyed some alone time at home.)

It takes some planning and flexibility, but there are ways to spend extra time with the people who matter most. For example, if I have an early flight, I'll drive my youngest son, Daniel, to school on the way to the airport. Or if my return flight lands when Daniel's school day ends, I'll pick him up on the way home and we'll grab a burger together. Similarly, if I am working downtown and have a speech later that evening, I'll ask Suzie and Shannon to meet me when they finish work, and we'll all have an early dinner together.

For the last three summers, Diane, who is studying to be a registered nurse, has worked the night shift at Evanston Hospital. Often, I'll stay up late and drive her to work at midnight, or I'll come by at seven-thirty in the morning to pick her up and bring her home. These times in the car give us an extra chance to connect.

When I travel domestically or internationally, whether I'm attending a board meeting or giving a speech, I always let Julie know several weeks in advance to see if she can join me. If so, we tack on an extra day before or after the event so we can spend more time together.

Does it take planning to work out the logistics? Yes, but having more ways to maximize my time with family is always worth the effort.

KNOWING HOW TO SAY NO

This brings us to choices *within* the family bucket. You can't possibly say yes to every invitation. The same planning and prioritization we discuss in chapter 5 must be applied here as well to decide which family events and functions you must attend and which ones are simply not a priority.

When we were first married, Julie and I seriously considered moving back to Minnesota because we were driving there once a month to spend weekends with our families. As we talked about it, we realized that if we were local, we'd face a lot of pressure to be at every birthday party and other family gatherings. We'd end up upsetting people and causing ourselves a lot of stress. Instead, every time we made the effort to come up from Chicago, people were so happy to see us. They understood that we couldn't attend every party or family dinner, and we made a sincere effort to get to some of the special events. Reflecting on this made the decision a lot easier: we stayed in Chicago!

Anna Budnik, whose story I shared in chapter 6, was candid about how she has come to terms over the years with having a busy career as an executive at Willis Towers Watson, being married with two children, and having a very large extended family. "My dad was one of 11, so I had about 30 cousins. This made for many birthday parties when I was growing up. Then I met my husband, who is one of ten children, and there were even more parties and get-togethers," Anna explained.

With so many cousins, nieces, and nephews (and now their children), Anna said it was easy to fall into what she called "Italian guilt" if she didn't attend every party. "But at some point, you have to prioritize," she added.

Anna shared a recent story of being invited to a birthday party for a one-year-old in the extended family. She also had been given Chicago Bears tickets for that same day and wanted to take her immediate family to the game. Her decision was to send a card and gift to the birthday party, with a promise to visit the relatives later in the week. That way she could go to the Bears game and enjoy the day without regret or guilt. "It's not saying no—it's making both work," she said.

Here's some advice that has helped me over the years. When you are trying to juggle numerous invitations and obligations— birthdays, weddings, and graduations—it's easy to make it all about you. You're wondering whether you'll be missed and what would happen if you don't show up. If you make it about other people instead, it's easier to choose when to accept an invitation and when it's okay to pass. If your presence is really important to the other person, and if being there feels like the right thing to do, that will heavily influence your decision. If at all possible, you're going to be there. However, if no one will really notice whether you're among the 300 guests at your fourth cousin's wedding, then it's probably just fine to send a gift and a card with your best wishes.

At times, though, there will be difficult choices to make. As my parents got older, I wanted to spend as much time as possible with them, while also pursuing balance in other areas of my life. I would often go to Minneapolis on my free weekends to see them, but not every weekend. I can remember one particular weekend when the children wanted to know if we could go to New York to see a Broadway play. As I self-reflected, I asked myself, "How would I feel if my parents passed away the week after I went to New York?" I acknowledged that I had gone to see my parents two weekends before. Even if that turned out to be my last visit, I was at peace. With that, I could make the decision to go to New York and, God willing, to see my parents again the next time I had a free weekend.

There will be trade-offs. Sometimes you can make the logistics work and sometimes you can't. Carol, a young woman I spoke to recently, shared with me her sadness of not being able to go home to Tennessee for Thanksgiving because her fiancé had to work the next day. "It just didn't make sense for us," she told me. Her decision was to engage in a new tradition that is gaining popularity among people who cannot be with their families for holidays: Friendsgiving. As the name implies, it is a gathering of friends and sometimes friends-of-friends around a holiday table. "I've never cooked a Thanksgiving meal before," Carol told me.

Rather than feeling excluded from her family, she engaged them long distance. "My mom and my aunts have been giving me their recipes. Mom and I are going to Skype on Thanksgiving morning so she can help me with the turkey," Carol said.

It's also important to acknowledge that there can be other circumstances that prevent people from spending time with their families. For some, their desire to live a healthy, values-based life is undermined by family issues. Instead of moving them toward life balance, interactions with certain members of their family threaten that balance. These relationships cause so much trauma that people must limit the amount of time they spend with some family members for the sake of their physical and mental health.

Self-reflection is the only way to make these difficult choices about what is the right thing to do. Getting support from others can help, especially people who can act as a sounding board to talk through the decision process and provide an outside perspective. Rather than feeling cut off, people who feel the stress of estranged or broken family relationships can find connections and meaning in other supportive relationships.

THE IMPORTANCE OF FRIENDSHIPS

Beyond our immediate family, there are other close relationships that enhance our lives.

Oprah Winfrey, in describing her sense of family, wrote in the February 2019 issue of her magazine, "Biologically, mine is pretty small. One sister, three nieces, a nephew. But emotionally and physically, the family keeps expanding. Looking around our Thanksgiving table last year, I was reminded of what it means to create bonds and relationships that bind you to the heart of yourself."[1]

From our core of family, we move to the first concentric circle of friends. These are the people who contribute to our sense of belonging, comfort, and sanctuary—and where, how, and to whom we give the same. By the time we're school-age, we're making friends. Most of us can think back to kindergarten and first grade when some boy or girl asked, "Do you want to be my friend?" Maybe you came home and announced to your parents that someone in your class told you, "You're my best friend." These early experiences taught us the importance of developing and maintaining friendships.

Even today, I stay in close touch with several high school friends. In fact, during our annual family vacation road trip last summer—the main purpose of which was to visit colleges with Daniel—we made a detour so I could show my children where I went to high school in Clarks Summit, Pennsylvania. We also stopped to see one of my high school friends. My children really enjoyed hearing stories about what I was like as a teenager.

From my college days, I have maintained close friendships with about a half-dozen guys. We get together every year for a long weekend to talk about life now versus then. We think back to when we first met, at age 17 or 18, and how much has changed (as well as what hasn't) 47 years later.

I've also made friends through various groups and activities, including church and Little League baseball. I even stay in touch with someone I met while sharing a cab in New York City. This collection of people from all walks of life is an important part of who I am.

As you reflect on your friendships, consider the people who are part of your memories and help tie your life together. Long-term friendships are an important constant in your life because these are the people who knew you when. When you want to celebrate, when you need support, when you need a listening ear, your friends are there for you, just as you try to be there for them.

Given my schedule, I'm often asked how I find time to keep in touch with so many people. Allow me to share a little secret: I stay in touch with brief, but frequent, conversations. These enable me to catch up, even if only for five or ten minutes. This is possible because I call friends every few weeks. When I'm driving downtown from my house and I know it's going to take an hour, I make several phone calls. If I'm in an airport and my flight gets delayed, I'll do the same thing. Even if I can't spend a lot of time, I show that I'm thinking of them.

These short check-ins keep friendships alive until you can get together in person. If you are not in touch frequently, though, you can't have a five-minute check-in. It would take an hour, which you probably don't have. So you put off calling, then it's been three months, six months, a year. The longer it goes between calls, the easier it is to lose touch.

Make a list of whom you need to contact and reach out to them. Once you catch up, commit to check in more often, but briefly (they're busy, too). When you make it a priority, you'll make these calls. And when you find yourself sitting at an airport gate because your flight has been delayed, you won't get annoyed or angry. You'll take out your phone and your list and catch up with friends who will be happy to hear from you.

BUILDING YOUR COMMUNITY

Returning to the image of concentric circles, the outer ring is community. I think about community on two levels. First, there are the people with whom we share meaningful experiences or engage in enriching activities. In 1986, David W. McMillan and David M. Chavis coined the seminal definition of *sense of community* as "a feeling that members have of belonging, a feeling that members matter to one another and to the group, and a shared faith that members' needs will be met through commitment to be together." Their definition applies to communities of every type, from neighborhoods to professional or spiritual groups.

Julie and I are very active in our faith community that comes together every Sunday to pray. I also have a sense of community at Kellogg, including colleagues I admire and many I consider to be close friends. There are other communities that I am part of less frequently but that are still very important to me. Every year for the past 40 years, I have attended a three-day silent retreat.

I go the first week of December, without fail. I'm joined by the same men every year. I would never go at another time, because that's "our week." No matter that I don't know these men—we can't even talk with each other (it's a silent retreat, as I discuss in chapter 10). I share a communal experience with them that is so important to who I am as a person.

In the same way, you share interests or life experiences with others. This could be a 12-step program, a study group, a book club, or a yoga class. There are even communal experiences that we enjoy unconsciously, such as when we're part of a group of fans at a baseball game, a concert, or a movie. When it's a shared experience, it adds to our joy.

As you self-reflect, think about the activities you enjoy that enrich your life. By sharing these experiences with others—whether through a club, a class, or another group—you can expand your sense of community. In the company of like-minded individuals, you can find more meaning, as well as fun.

THE WORKPLACE AS A COMMUNITY

Another important community for many people is the workplace. It makes sense because many people spend the bulk of their week-days working. Whether that occurs in a work setting such as an office or we work virtually, we are in constant contact with the same group of people every day. When this is a positive connection, it adds to our sense of community. We belong!

It's no surprise that it's far more rewarding to work with people you respect and who feel the same way about you. As research shows, positive work friendships not only make work more enjoyable but also help people be more successful. "Warm, positive relationships are important at work for very human reasons," Annie McKee, a senior fellow at the University of Pennsylvania Graduate School of Education, wrote in *Harvard Business Review*. "Since the beginning of time, people have organized into tribes that labor and play together. Today organizations are our tribes. We want to work in a group or a company that makes us proud and inspires us to give our best efforts."[3]

Having mutual respect for and alignment with your colleagues goes to the heart of what I call a *best team*. In my second book, *Becoming the Best: Build a World-Class Organization through Values-Based Leadership,* I describe five bests: best self, best team, best partner, best investment, and best citizen. On a personal level, being a values-based leader and committing to lead a values-based life is the heart of being your best self.

When we interact with others, as we do in any community including the workplace, we are part of a best team. A best team is formed when people are self-reflective, understand themselves, and come together with a sense of common purpose. In fact, it takes every individual operating at his or her best self for the group to function at its best. To clarify this point, I don't mean a collection of superstars, like some elite team of highly paid professional athletes. Rather, a best team is a group of people who have the capability and desire to work well together, so that the collective efforts of the team are far greater than what any individual can contribute on his or her own.

At the heart of the best team are commonly held values. This is the basis of building the team to ensure that everyone is pulling in the same direction. A similar sentiment was echoed in a discussion I had about community and leading a values-based life with Jeffrey M. Solomon, chairman and CEO of Cowen Inc., a publicly traded, independent investment bank with more than 100 years of history. (Jeff also shares more of his story in chapter 10.)

Jeff describes his firm as a community, brought together by common goals and objectives, at the center of which are shared values: vision, empathy, sustainability, and tenacious teamwork—or VEST. Although each team member contributes differently, having a vision brings them all together. Vision also fosters innovation as opportunities and challenges are anticipated.

Empathy fosters engagement with others to understand where people are coming from—their needs and desires. With empathy, a culture is created in which people care about each other and truly want to help each other be successful.

The value of sustainability speaks to both profitability and having a positive impact. "Internally within Cowen and externally in the community, sustainability benefits us—and not just from a profitability standpoint," Jeff explained. "The more good we can do for ourselves, the more good we can do for the world. That's the concept of sustainability."

Jeff's observation reminded me of a comment I heard years ago from Baxter chairman William Graham, who used to say, "Aren't we blessed to be able to do well by doing good?"

Cowen, like every other business, needs to generate a return for its shareholders. However, sustainability also acknowledges that building relationships for the long term is more important than making as much profit as possible in the short term. With sustainability as a value, the emphasis is still on making a "fair return and getting paid for providing a service," Jeff said. "But we also have to be willing to leave something on the table. We can't be doing things that jeopardize relationships longer term."

This echoed the concept of best partner as I describe in *Becoming the Best*. Best partnerships are holistic, guided by collaboration and mutual respect, instead of trying to squeeze every dime out of every transaction. Partnerships benefit all involved, becoming a competitive advantage and ultimately enabling all parties to achieve more profitability and work together to satisfy customers and grow their businesses in a highly competitive environment.

Cowen's value of "tenacious teamwork" defines how people work together in the community, as individuals who collaborate. "We believe that the problems we are trying to solve are complex and require more than one person to come up with a valuable solution," Jeff said. "If someone isn't willing to work with others, [he or she is] not going to work at Cowen."

A challenge for leaders in creating a best team is helping individuals see the impact of their efforts. Too often, people focus too narrowly only on what they do. When they can see how what they do affects the team, the department, and the entire company—no matter how big or small that impact—they begin to see themselves as part of a bigger whole. They're in a community in which everyone plays an important part.

As we discussed in chapter 6, having supportive relationships at work enables people to be honest about what they have going on in their lives and to find ways to pursue balance. This is a community that can truly bring out the best in people.

CELEBRATING THE BROADER COMMUNITY

Now let's take a look at a broader sense of community, which is not limited to neighbors, the workplace, or any other institutional or spiritual group. On the highest level, community is defined by everyone with whom we come in contact. I practice this sense of community by saying hello and exchanging a few words with everyone I meet during the day. Every time I walk into Kellogg's Global Hub, I make it a point to speak with the receptionists, Chris and Kenn. It's not just a nice or polite thing to do, it's important to me, and they've become my good friends.

I also look for ways to brighten someone's day. For example, when I am a guest speaker at an event at a hotel and am given a bottle of wine, rather than put it in my suitcase, I make it a gift to the taxi driver who takes me to the airport.

Everyone matters: the people you see in the elevator, in the company or school cafeteria, in the hotel lobby, on the airplane—everywhere. We are all part of a community defined by our humanness. We're not the same—we are individuals. We have different opinions and beliefs. In this regard, I've always followed the Prayer of St. Francis that reminds us of the importance of seeking first to understand rather than to be understood and to love instead of being loved.

If we want to enjoy a strong community, we need to acknowledge our differences and to celebrate them in the spirit of inclusion. At the same time, we need to celebrate all the things that make us the same: the desire to do good, to provide for our families and loved ones, to have purpose and meaning.

All people, no matter who they are or where they come from, are our sisters and brothers. In any way I can, small or large, I try to feel part of that big, global community. Within a broad community, no one is left behind. We all belong. We all matter.

NEXT STEPS TO BETTER BALANCE

Given the importance of family, friends, and community, reflect on the following:

- What beliefs and values have you gained from your family of origin or your extended family?
- How does family enable you keep a sense of balance?
- When and where do you have conflicts between your family life bucket and your other commitments?
- Make a list of your family members and friends. Who haven't you talked to in a while? Who can you reach out to reconnect with today or this week?
- What communities are you part of, whether you share an affiliation or a meaningful activity?
- What can you do to brighten the lives of the people you interact with every day?

CHAPTER 8

HEALTH: THE ALL-PURPOSE BUCKET

O f all the life buckets, health is the one that, at some point in your life, will demand your attention. When you're not aware of how out of balance you've become, this bucket will give you a warning. It may be that you notice a number on the scale that surprises you. Among my circle of friends and associates, I know of several who, amid intense times in their careers, gained 30 to 50 pounds, or more. At the time, they were surprised. As they began to self-reflect on their work schedules, travel, business dinners, and lack of exercise, however, they had to ask themselves the question from chapter 2, "Why am I surprised?"

You may receive another kind of warning, such as exhaustion after putting in too many all-nighters to get a project done. Sleep deprivation, as we discuss later in this chapter, is a serious health issue and not a badge of honor. Or, after your annual physical examination, your doctor may have a surprising report for you (but, again, why are you surprised?): high blood pressure, elevated cholesterol levels, or a prediabetes warning. If you don't pay attention, you may hit the wall (as discussed in chapter 3) with something more serious, like a heart attack.

It's so easy for us to fool ourselves, at least for a little while. We tell ourselves that we can take care of our health later. When things slow down and we're not working so much, or when the children are older, we'll adopt better eating habits and exercise more. Although we acknowledge that we should stop smoking, we tell ourselves it's just too stressful to quit right now. And yes, maybe we have been drinking a little too much lately, but it's all those dinners with clients and customers. Besides, after a long day, who doesn't deserve a beer or a scotch (or two or three . . .)?

The truth is, if you don't pay attention to your health now, you'll face the consequences later. That's a price no one should have to pay. No job, no promotion, no amount of money is worth the cost to your health. This is hardly a new idea. Two thousand years ago, the Roman poet Virgil wrote, "The greatest wealth is health."

As I reflect on health, I know what a blessing it is. Having reached an age at which friends and peers have faced serious health issues and some have passed away, I try always to be conscious about my health. I thank God (literally) every day that I wake up, put both feet on the floor, and move through the day with physical energy and mental alertness—knowing that there will be a day when that will no longer happen. Although that might sound a little morbid, it's a reminder that none of us should take our health for granted. Health is a gift, and it's up to us to decide how we're going to use it.

IN OUR YOUNGER DAYS

Health seemed much simpler when we were young. We didn't think about exercise, we just ran around outdoors. We didn't train at the gym, we played games at the park.

When I was growing up in Pennsylvania, my family's house was behind the baseball park at school. Every summer morning,

10 to 15 children from the neighborhood—anywhere from first to eighth or ninth grade—would show up at about nine o'clock in the morning for pickup games. We divided ourselves into teams and played until we had to go home for lunch, and then we returned to the park to play baseball all afternoon. After that, it was time for Little League. By the time I went to bed that night, I had played baseball for almost 12 hours.

I still played baseball in high school and started playing tennis. Both sports kept me active and allowed me to spend time with my friends. Then I got to college. Between classes and studying, there wasn't as much time for athletics. That's when, as I relate in chapter 4, my roommate and I decided to start running. From then on, jogging became my preferred way to exercise—fast, efficient, and enjoyable.

There have been times, though, when making time for exercise was challenging. After I graduated from college, I worked full-time and had frequent business travel. Plus, every other weekend, I drove up to my alma mater to visit Julie, who was then my girlfriend, and I helped my parents when they needed me. With all that going on, it seemed a little selfish to be thinking about exercise because I viewed it as something I did solely for myself. By the time I got into my thirties, however, I noticed some of my friends and associates were starting to have health issues, which sometimes caused them to miss work. This was a wake-up call for me: if I wanted to be the best I could be in every area of my life, I had to pay more attention to my health. It wasn't selfish at all. Having life balance in work, family, spirituality, and giving back would only be possible if I stayed healthy.

Health is unique among all the life buckets because it affects every other aspect of your life. To share a quote that's a favorite of my friend Kent Thiry, executive chairman and former CEO of DaVita, Inc., a leading kidney dialysis company, and an avid athlete, "One cannot pour from an empty cup." If you don't take care of your health, how can you take care of others?

THE CORPORATE ATHLETE

I've also come to appreciate that health isn't just taking a walk or eating more vegetables. It's holistic, comprising every aspect of my life: physical, emotional, mental, and spiritual. I came to a deeper understanding of this concept nearly 20 years ago, when I was given the *Harvard Business Review* article "The Making of a Corporate Athlete" by Jim Loehr and Tony Schwartz. It had a big impact on me then, and I continue to use it in my Kellogg classes today.

The authors' premise is that everyone in the workplace must be a "corporate athlete"; in order to be successful, they must train in "the same systematic, multilevel way that world-class athletes do." Rather than relying on "brain power" alone, the authors explain, high performance needs to be viewed as a pyramid with four levels:

1. At the base is physical wellness, which promotes endurance and allows for mental and emotional resilience.
2. The second level is emotional, to create a more positive emotional state.
3. The third level is mental capacity, to be able to channel physical and mental energy into what needs to be done.
4. The fourth level is spiritual capacity, which reinforces motivation, determination, and endurance.

The authors' conclusion is as timely today as it was eye-opening nearly two decades ago: "On the playing field or in the boardroom, high performance depends as much on how people renew and recover energy as on how they expend it, on how they manage their lives as much as how they manage their work."[1]

I resonated with the four-level approach to health: physical, emotional, mental, and spiritual. I began to connect this approach to health to my practice of daily self-reflection. As I asked myself how I was living my values—with my family, in my work, in my faith, and in my interactions with others—I also needed to reflect on how I was taking care of my health with the habits and routines that make the most sense to me.

MAKING HEALTH A PRIORITY

Yes, you only have 168 hours a week, so exercising, eating more nutritiously, getting more sleep, and relaxing and recharging your energy may—once again—seem like something you can't afford to do. Where will this time come from? I can't tell you how many times people tell me, "Harry, I would exercise more, but I just don't have time." What they're really saying is, "It's not a priority for me." People who pursue balance in their lives know that health must be a priority, and that includes exercise. Whether it's yoga, going for a walk, taking a run, riding a bicycle, swimming, or any other physical activity, exercise is good for body, mind, and soul.

Anna Budnik (see chapters 6 and 7) has an incredibly busy work and family life, and she still devotes time to running and lifting weights. "If I have calls very early in the morning with colleagues in Europe and then a gap before my next meeting, I'll take a one-hour run," Anna told me. "When I travel, there'd better be a gym—that's the number one criterion for any hotel. Exercising helps me relieve stress."

I couldn't agree more. When I travel, I try to stay in hotels that have a 24-hour gym. If I arrive late or I have all-day meetings, I want at least 45 minutes on a treadmill or elliptical at night. There are times, though, when I have to make other arrangements, such as on a recent trip to New York to give a speech. I was all set to go to the fitness center when I discovered it closed at 9 p.m. Instead of giving up and going back to my room, I took a six-mile walk around Manhattan. While I was walking, I made some phone calls and caught up with a few friends. That activity helped me clear my mind and think about the next day. I returned to my room, refreshed and calm. I read and sent emails for about an hour, did my nightly self-reflection, then got ready for bed and slept soundly until it was time to get up the next morning.

And by the way, over the years I've noticed how health is one life bucket that gives dividends on the time and energy I invest in it. The healthier and more active I am, the more energy and focus I have.

SLEEP: IT'S NOT OPTIONAL

Sleep is just as crucial to your health as exercise, yet you may be tempted to convince yourself that it is not important. Maybe it's a habit you got into in high school or college, when you pulled an all-nighter to finish that term paper. (As we discussed in chapter 5, being planful probably would have helped then—and it certainly helps now.) Maybe you view lack of sleep as an indication of how busy and important you are. That kind of thinking, though, is not only unhealthy, it's also unsustainable.

A recent study, for example, found that "sleep devaluation" was shockingly common among some leaders who sent that message to their teams. As Christopher M. Barnes wrote in *Harvard Business Review* in 2018, "They may do this by setting an example (for instance, boasting about sleeping only four hours or sending work emails at 3 AM), or they may directly shape employees' habits by encouraging people to work during typical sleep hours (perhaps criticizing subordinates for not responding to those 3 AM emails, or praising individuals who regularly work late into the night)."[2]

If your job is the cause of chronic sleeplessness, then you need to address this problem before it takes a toll on your health. For example, Arianna Huffington, the founder of *The Huffington Post*, became a vocal sleep advocate after she admitted to collapsing from severe sleep deprivation. In an interview with CNBC, Huffington called it a "complete delusion" for someone to assume that getting little sleep and not taking care of themselves will somehow make them more productive. "You can succeed much more effectively, and much more sustainably, and with much less damage to your health and your relationships," she said.[3]

If you're still telling yourself that you only need four hours (or less) of sleep (plus multiple shots of espresso each day), then consider this advice from Barnes in *Harvard Business Review:* better sleep contributes to success. As the article states, "It is clear that you can squeeze in more work hours if you sleep less. But remember that the quality of your work—and your leadership—inevitably declines as you do so, often in ways that are invisible to you."[4] Although the article focuses on leaders and their influence on teams, we can just as easily apply these findings to ourselves and our influence on family, friends, and colleagues. When we're well rested, we're more likely to be even-tempered, have more patience, listen better, and engage well with others. When we're sleep-deprived to the point of exhaustion, the opposite occurs—and everyone feels it.

Beyond the impact on your physical health, sleep deprivation can also drag on your emotions, motivation, energy level, and general outlook on life. According to the National Sleep Foundation, "If you're feeling low, you may not realize that lack of sleep is the culprit. But even small levels of sleep deprivation over time can chip away at your happiness. You might see that you're less enthusiastic, more irritable, or even have some of the symptoms of clinical depression, such as feeling persistently sad or empty."[5]

The bottom line here is sleep is not optional. You may find that six hours is optimal for you or you may need eight hours. The more self-aware you are, the more you can gauge your health and need for sleep—and with better clarity than if you're running on fumes and caffeine.

YOUR MENTAL HEALTH

This brings up another very important issue: mental health. It's beyond the scope of this chapter to give mental health the in-depth attention it deserves. According to the National Institute of Mental Health, mental illnesses affect tens of millions of people in the US alone. Yet it is estimated that only about half of people with mental illnesses receive treatment. Within the broad category of mental illnesses, the most common are anxiety disorders, affecting about 40 million adults (age 18 and older) in the US. Although highly treatable, only a little more than one-third of those who suffer from anxiety disorders receive treatment.[6]

I share these few statistics here in hopes of joining a much broader discussion in society to normalize how we talk about and address mental illness. There has been a stigma about mental illness for far too long; yet, if we're honest with ourselves, we can admit that we or our loved ones have been affected by a mental illness such as depression, anxiety, or mood disorder.

As the discussion on the corporate athlete reminds us, emotional and mental health are key components to our overall well-being. Loehr and Schwartz observe, "Just as positive emotions ignite the energy that drives high performance, negative emotions—frustration, impatience, anger, fear, resentment, and sadness—drain energy . . . Anxious, fear-ridden athletes are far more likely to choke in competition, for example, while anger and frustration sabotage their capacity for calm focus. The impact of negative emotions on business performance is subtler but no less devastating."[7]

Our mental health can go unchecked for a while if we aren't being self-reflective. Many mental health issues begin to develop as life becomes more complex. Job stress and family stress can trigger or contribute to episodes of depression. With daily self-reflection, you will more closely monitor your emotional and mental health, just as you become more aware of your physical health. By asking yourself questions such as "Am I really feeling my best?" and "Are there health issues I'm concerned about but not addressing?" you will begin to acknowledge what you need for support in living a more balanced life. That support may include seeing a medical doctor or psychiatrist, talking with a therapist or a counselor, seeking the advice of a clergyperson, or talking with family or friends. Meditation, prayer, and other spiritual practices, as we discuss in chapter 10, can also positively contribute to mental and emotional health.

Do not shortchange yourself on the help you need. That starts with becoming self-reflective so you can continually monitor your health: physical, emotional, mental, and spiritual. Then, with greater self-awareness, you can identify the kinds of lifelong habits that will help you become healthier and experience more balance in your life.

CREATING LIFETIME HABITS

The earlier we build healthy habits, the better it is for us. For one, we realize the benefits of healthier living from a young age. The other reason is it's harder to build healthy habits later in life—although it's never too late. I know people who began exercising in their forties and fifties, and people in their late sixties who quit smoking after 50 years. Breaking a lifetime of poor habits may be tough, but with your health at stake, you've got a great incentive.

As I get older, I am more aware of the importance of taking care of my health and staying as active as possible. Once people hit 80 years old, the top cause of death is from a fall. This isn't because a fall is particularly deadly, but because the time spent in recovery at a hospital can lead to other complications, including pneumonia. Knowing this, I make sure that I go to the gym and do my daily stretches because I want to minimize health risks from falls and injuries as I get older.

Building habits for better health may seem daunting at first, but these habits are built slowly over a long period of time. Just as we discussed in chapter 4, we can't adopt someone else's habits for health and self-care and decide that will work for us. Some people thrive with yoga; others have no interest. Running may be exhilarating for one person and drudgery for another. I was reminded of this the other day when I was speaking with a friend of mine who works in hospice. For her, daily yoga and monthly massages are crucial elements of her self-care. For her husband, she added, "That would be torture. If you gave him a gift certificate for a massage, he wouldn't use it."

My friend's perspective is important as we look at examples of how other people have made deep commitments to improving and sustaining their health. Their stories may resonate with you, or you may find them interesting but not directly applicable. The purpose is not to be prescriptive, but I hope to inspire you to consider how you, too, can become more engaged in your health bucket.

THE FITNESS PROJECT

I'm fortunate to know several corporate athletes who take a holistic, physical-emotional-mental-spiritual approach to health. Among them is Carter Cast, my friend and colleague whose story I shared in chapters 3 and 4. While an undergraduate student at Stanford University in the early 1980s, Carter was an All-American swimmer. However, during a period of life imbalance, as he described in chapter 3, Carter faced health issues including being 30 pounds overweight, having heart arrhythmia, and needing stomach surgery to address debilitating acid reflux. Confronted with this reality, he realized he couldn't remember the last time he exercised.

As part of his pathway back toward life balance, Carter gave himself what he called a "side project"—a phrase he picked up from his dad, who had always been engaged in projects that interested him. One of Carter's side projects was swimming across a lake in Indiana, a distance of about 10,000 yards or roughly six miles. Back in his college days, Carter would have conquered that distance with ease. After so many years, though, the lake swim was a challenge—physically, emotionally, and mentally. Recognizing the magnitude of the challenge, Carter made it a project with interim goals that he reflected on and journaled about on a regular basis.

His first training swim—on January 2, 2019—was 750 yards, after which he recorded in his journal that he "felt pretty awful." Two weeks later, he made it 1,000 yards, and then 1,200 yards in February, after which he recorded still feeling awful, but less so than in January. Little by little, Carter increased his distance and logged his progress, keeping himself accountable to his milestones as well as his feelings.

Carter recalled an experience early on in his training, of swimming in a lane next to someone who was outpacing him. "He was killing me. When I got home, I said to my wife, 'I don't think this is going to happen.' It's like I have lost myself. I'm not that guy anymore." His wife listened with compassion, then reminded him of a simple truth he'd lost sight of. She told him, "Carter, you haven't done a swim like this in 25 or 30 years. You have to be patient."

Her feedback changed Carter's perspective. Instead of swimming on the clock, timing every lap the way he did at Stanford, he just swam. "Time-based swimming was pulling me down. I was being my harshest critic," Carter explained. "So I stopped competing against the 'old self' I had been in college, and just focused on slowly increasing my distance per workout and building momentum."

Although swimming is a solitary endeavor, Carter didn't take on this side project alone. He found two former swimmers who were triathletes—one in North Carolina and one in Chicago—to join him in the lake swim challenge. They trained separately, kept each other appraised of their progress via text messages, and committed to swim across the lake together in July 2019. When that day finally came, it started out as an amicable swim across the lake, each swimmer encouraging the others. Then as the opposite shore neared, Carter felt his old competitive spirit rekindle. With a friendly apology to his companions, Carter explained he just had to go for it. With their approval and encouragement, he raced the final mile to the other side.

Carter's sense of accomplishment reflected far more than the six miles he swam that day. The victory was channeling positive self-talk and building self-confidence during seven months of training while gradually extending his distance and increasing his endurance.

THE LIFELONG ATHLETE

Another corporate athlete I'm proud to know is Mike Zafirovski, a former executive at General Electric and Motorola, former CEO of Nortel, and an executive advisor to The Blackstone Group. A lifelong athlete, Mike has been a runner since he was a teenager and completed his first marathon at the age of 24. In 2018, at the age of 65, he completed the Kona Ironman Triathlon. An Ironman Triathlon is a series of long-distance, multisport races—each of which would be an incredible accomplishment, and combined are mind-boggling: a 2.4-mile swim, a 112-mile bicycle ride, concluding with a 26.2-mile marathon.

Growing up in Macedonia, Mike played soccer as a youngster. After emigrating to the US, he took up swimming in high school (his school didn't have a soccer team) and later attended college on a swimming scholarship. These activities formed a lifelong discipline to stay physically fit and to pursue balance amid the work pressures. "I realized that, when I ran, I felt 100 times better. When I was working 12 hours a day, sports became a complement to that. I felt better and got rid of any anxiety I was feeling," Mike recalled.

As Mike's career advanced and he became a leader, his passion for physical activity became part of his leadership—not as a competitor, but as a role model. "I used to encourage people to exercise. Over lunch, I'd go running. In time, I had 25 or more people running with me."

This team approach extended to Mike's family life. "When my oldest son was five years old, he would come with me, riding his bike while I ran." Later, his sons and his wife would join him on long runs. Mike competed in his first Ironman in 2002 and since then has completed three Ironman competitions.

As impressive as Mike's athletic accomplishments are, he is the first to point out that it's not necessary for someone to be an extreme athlete to be active. "Walking is the best exercise," he said, echoing the encouragement he frequently gives to others.

His comment brings to mind my own practices when I was at Baxter, which has a beautiful corporate campus with walking paths. I noticed that few people ever took advantage of those paths. During the nice weather, instead of meeting in my office, I'd often invite colleagues to take a walk with me and discuss topics along the way. The combination of fresh air and exercise energized us and often led to more creative brainstorming. Over time, I noticed, we were setting a good example as more people began walking those paths.

Once again, it's a reminder that taking care of our health—in terms of nutrition, sleep, physical exercise, mindfulness, and spiritual practice—is not just for ourselves alone. We're role models for those around us, encouraging them to consider how they, too, might address their health. By engaging with others, it becomes a team sport—one that can enhance all our other life buckets.

HEALTH AS A TEAM SPORT

Whether at work or among family and friends, we want to engage with others in fun activities that we have in common. For example, while I was at Baxter, we created softball teams to encourage team building at all levels, from executives to summer interns. While on the baseball field, we weren't titles—we were people. I can remember showing up for a game between two Baxter teams in my jeans, T-shirt, and a baseball cap. When I'd be tagged out on a close play or run for a fly ball and someone crashed into me, I'd hear someone say, "Hey, maybe you shouldn't be so tough on the CEO." Inevitably, a person who was new to the company would call someone else aside and ask, "That's not really the CEO, is it?" No doubt that newcomer would get clued in, but at that moment I was only Harry Kraemer, baseball team member.

Kent Thiry, whose favorite quote opened this chapter, takes a very active approach to team building. An avid hiker and biker, he embraces these activities as the center of his life and his well-being—and he regularly encourages family, friends, and team members to join him. Every year for the past ten years, Kent has taken a group from DaVita on excursions into nature. About half these events involve mountain biking, with participants who range from beginners to more experienced riders. At the end of the day, the group sits around a campfire and contemplates introspective questions.

"People open up remarkably," Kent told me. "There are some very serious conversations. Then we switch to singing around the campfire."

Kent has engaged in the same outings—mixing outdoor activity, introspection, and bonding—with his family members. For years, he has taken trips with his son and his son's friends, which include "office hours" he holds with each of the young people to talk about anything that's on their minds—personal or professional. For the past 24 years in a row, Kent and his siblings have gotten together for a long weekend at the family cottage in Wisconsin. "We keep notes each year of our goals so that we each have to face up to the stuff we keep saying, but never change," he explained.

Although these activities are shared with others, they are grounded in Kent's personal practices, which include exercise, personal journaling, Buddhist readings, time spent outdoors, and periods of quiet reflection. "I am very healthy about 85 percent of the time, and unhealthy about 15 percent of the time," Kent admitted. "So I use journaling and tracking my progress to stay objective."

PURSUING HEALTH HOLISTICALLY

Importantly, as Kent observed, these activities are not just about physical fitness. The goal is to experience greater health holistically: addressing the four dimensions of physical, emotional, mental, and spiritual health. "These practices are essential to me—body and soul," he said. "For example, when I travel, the first thing that gets scheduled every day is when I will exercise. That's not an option."

For Kent, as with so many of us, exercise and physical activity are not just habits; they are part of the rituals that touch multiple aspects of our lives. As Loehr and Schwartz described in "The Making of a Corporate Athlete," such rituals foster better balance by allowing disengagement from work and tapping into a deeper sense of purpose and meaning: "Rituals that give people the opportunity to pause and look inside include meditation, journal writing, prayer, and service to others. Each of these activities can also serve as a source of recovery—a way to break the linearity of relentless goal-oriented activity."[8]

For some, these rituals may involve hiking and contemplating the beauty of nature and the grandeur of creation. For others, it may be a long walk or run, combined with listening to podcasts of inspiring sermons or lectures or time for prayer and contemplation. On the surface, it may seem like multitasking, but it's deeper than that. Body, mind, and spirit are fully engaged through movement, thought, and contemplation.

THE BUCKET CONNECTION

The activities we love can be enhanced by sharing them with family and friends. I love bike riding with my family, especially in the fall when the leaves are turning. In the winter months, we go skiing together—even with a day trip to Wisconsin where the runs may be down hills instead of mountains, but there is no shortage of fun. We take walks together on a spring or summer day, just like I did as a child with my grandfather. Or, when I'm going to the gym to work out, Julie or one (or more) of the children will often join me. We'll work out together on the ellipticals, talking as we get our exercise.

Taking a walk or run by yourself can be part of your spiritual practice as it also promotes your health. Taking that same walk or run with another person can also reinforce your family and other personal relationships. Equally important, the joy you feel from whatever you're doing—walking, running, biking, swimming, or any other activity—generates a sense of fun. This is the unique gift of the health bucket: it not only enhances but also engages other aspect of our lives. Over time, we're not only healthier—we're happier.

NEXT STEPS TO BETTER BALANCE

When it comes to health, self-awareness is crucial. We may be able to fool ourselves for a short time, but eventually health issues will catch up with us. As you self-reflect, consider these questions:

- Where do you want to make improvements in your health: diet/nutrition, exercise, sleep, or stress management?
- What habits and rituals do you currently engage in that help your health and well-being?
- What habits and rituals would you like to add?

- Do certain sports or other activities appeal to you?
- What goals can you set for yourself? What coaching or other support do you need?

Remember, health really is the greatest gift. The more you make it a priority for yourself, the greater your chances of enjoying that gift for the rest of your life.

CHAPTER 9

THE IMPORTANCE OF FUN

As we think about pursuing life balance, it makes sense that we allocate our time to significant life buckets such as work, family, and health—and, for many of us, to spirituality and making a difference as well. When we think about fun, however, we might question whether that's really a big enough priority to warrant having its own bucket. We may be tempted to sandwich fun into health (exercise can be fun, right?). Or we might think that it belongs in the bucket for family, friends, and community because that's probably who we are having fun with most of the time.

If that's your immediate reaction to having a fun bucket, think again. Fun should be viewed as far more than a distraction or as something that's nice to do when you have time—which you may never have. The fact is it is impossible for most of us to live a values-based life without also including fun. It really is that much of a priority.

The pursuit of life balance means that you're not overly concentrated in any one area. As you allocate your 168 into various buckets, you need a variety of activities and experiences, and that

151

includes fun. The old saying that warns against having all work and no play contains a lot of truth. There's even science behind it. Pleasant experiences such as playing, laughing, singing, and dancing trigger the release of chemicals produced in your brain, including endorphins that make you feel good. The adage that laughter is the best medicine gets an endorsement from no less than the Mayo Clinic.[1] Laughter is known to relieve stress, stimulate your lungs and heart, and improve circulation. Over time, laughter may even help your mood, relieve pain, and give you a better outlook on life.

Fun enriches our lives with experiences, often shared with others, such as watching a movie, going to a concert, or visiting a museum. Fun gives our bodies and minds a chance to relax and recharge; as a result, we're more likely to be alert, productive, and creative.

With a greater appreciation for the importance of fun (other than just being enjoyable!), let's look at what that means for your values-based life.

WHAT FUN MEANS TO YOU

When you were young, you probably didn't have to think twice about what it meant to have fun. Sports, games, riding a bicycle, playing with friends—any number of activities could fill a weekend and those long days during summer vacation. As an adult, though, you may find that fun is not as easily defined as it was when you were a child. In fact, if you've discovered in reading these pages that you're out of balance (and that happens to all of us—no judgment here), you may be out of practice when it comes to fun.

There's no prescription for what fun should look like, any more than anyone could tell you what to do for your health, personal relationships, or any other aspect of your life. It is *your* 168, after all. That said, it may be helpful to consider fun in seven categories. In reading these, you may find there is more opportunity to put fun in your life than you realized.

Planned Fun: Make It a Priority

As you recall from chapter 5, being planful in your life is essential for managing all aspects of your 168. Now we realize just how important being planful is for having more fun. If you want to experience more fun as part of your life balance, you can't leave it to chance. You need to plan for fun.

Here's how I think about it. With my 168, I am very focused on all the things I need to do. I allocate time for work, and I prioritize what absolutely must get done every day. I also make sure I'm spending meaningful time with my family, that I'm exercising and getting enough sleep, and I'm attending to my spiritual life (as we address in chapter 10). In addition (as we discuss in chapter 11), knowing that I'm only here for a short time, I want to make a positive impact in any way I can. Sounds like a lot, and it is; however, I can't forget about fun, which is key to pursuing life balance. In a column she wrote for *O, The Oprah Magazine* (which also appeared on Oprah.com), author and researcher Brené Brown emphasized the importance of scheduling unstructured time for fun. As she observed, "Play—doing things just because they're fun and not because they'll help achieve a goal—is vital to human development."[2]

One of the most important times for fun is vacation—taking a break from the daily routine and investing more time in personal relationships. I find it interesting, though, that many people don't take all their annual vacation. For some, it's like a badge of honor. Someone told me recently (and with a bit of pride in his voice) that when he retired, he had 19 weeks of accumulated vacation. That's nearly *five months* of vacation time not taken! Another friend told me that it had been "16 months since I had more than one day off." The exact number—16 months—meant she was keeping a count.

I had to wonder: was she keeping score? How was that helping her life balance?

If you feel guilty about taking time off because of your work responsibilities, think of it this way: paid vacation time is part of your compensation—one way your employer rewards you. So why wouldn't you take your vacation the same way you accept your paycheck and other benefits?

I worked very hard in my corporate career, including more than ten years combined as CFO and then CEO and chairman of Baxter International; however, I always made sure I took all of my vacation days. When I was just starting out and was entitled to two weeks of vacation, I took those two weeks. When my vacation time increased, I took all that vacation time every year, because I recognized that time away from the job actually benefited my performance. I recognized that I could not pursue balance as part of living a values-based life if I couldn't take time away from the office.

I also knew that when I was on vacation, I could spend more time with family, see friends, take care of my health, enjoy leisure activities, and devote extra time to prayer and self-reflection. Vacation time is crucial to improving my physical, emotional, mental, and spiritual health (as we discuss in chapter 8).

Now ask yourself: when was the last time you took a vacation—not just a day or two, but an entire week? If it's been longer than a year, perhaps it's time to do some self-reflection as to why. The culprit is probably work—and I understand that it can be hard to break away. If you let it, however, work will occupy all 168 hours of your week—52 weeks a year.

By giving up your vacation time, you're shortchanging yourself on life balance. You're missing out on opportunities to relax and recharge. As author Amy Hinote observed in her book *The Power of a Vacation,* each of us has a fundamental need to broaden our horizons and change our perspectives. "As human beings, we also have a need to escape our everyday lives," Hinote wrote.

"We crave leisurely mornings minus alarms. A fresh powdering of snow. Afternoons spent listening to the waves, our feet snuggled in sand and moonlit nights under starry skies."[3]

Although travel allows us to break from our daily routines, we can also engage in fun and leisurely activities closer to home. If your finances or other circumstances prevent you from making a trip right now, you can still reap the benefits of a change of pace. The walking or biking paths near your home can help you relax just as much as strolling the streets of London or the beaches of Hawaii.

A vacation, though, doesn't just happen. You need to plan, from scheduling days off from work to deciding what you're going to do with your free time. If you're planning to travel during your vacation, you obviously need to make arrangements. Even if you're taking a staycation, you still need to plan. What will you do during that time? If you've been saying that you wished you had more time for a favorite leisure activity, there is nothing like a vacation to give you that opportunity. If you fail to plan, however, you can get so wrapped up in work that you don't take your vacation. Maybe you'll squeeze in a day off or two by the end of the year, but there won't be enough weeks left to take all your vacation. You'll have to roll your unused vacation to the next year (if you can) or else you'll lose it.

Being planful is the only way to avoid that happening—and the earlier you start making those plans, the better. When my children were younger, my family vacation time was dictated largely by their school schedules and, later on, by summer jobs and summer school classes. Every year, in late July and early August, we take a two-week road trip, which I jokingly call our *Walley World* trip, after the road adventure in *National Lampoon's Vacation*.

Getting two adults and five children to our final destination, with various stops and side trips along the way, requires quite a bit of planning. Yet that's part of the fun. We plan from point A to point B, with flexibility to be spontaneous along the way.

Yes, it's an effort. The busier you are at work, the more challenging it will be to keep your commitment to yourself and your family to take that vacation—especially if you intend to unplug as much as possible. When I was at Baxter, there were many times when I worked up to the last minute before our departure on vacation. I can remember being at the office until very late on Friday night and even into the early hours of Saturday morning so I could finish everything before vacation. My office phone would ring well after midnight, and it would be Julie asking me, "Are you coming home?" By putting in that extra time, though, I could leave the office behind when the family packed up and hit the road.

Depending on what was going on, I sometimes had to make a few phone calls while we were away. I can remember when the children were young, locking myself in the hotel bathroom to take a conference call and my daughter Suzie wiggling her fingers under the door and asking, "Daddy, can you see my fingers? When are you taking me to the beach?" These days, I'm more likely to keep up with email while traveling—not all the time, usually in the evening after everyone else is asleep. I find a daily email check-in is preferable to dealing with two weeks of unread emails when I come back from vacation.

No matter how challenging it is to juggle the logistics, or how much work you'll face when you come back, don't let that stop you from taking a vacation. You owe it to yourself to have some planned fun.

Stress-Releasing Fun: It's Good for You!

If we go back to chapter 1, recall that one of the benefits of pursuing life balance is minimizing worry, fear, anxiety, pressure, and stress. A big part of that is being self-reflective to increase self-awareness of how we're feeling and what we need to pursue better balance. Often, what we need is more fun, particularly when we are feeling stressed.

Using myself as an example, when I have a big project that needs to get done in the next few days, I'll work several hours in a row without taking a break. After working nine or ten hours straight, I have to clear my head for a little while. Sometimes that means going for a jog, working out at the gym for an hour, or taking a bicycle ride with the family. Other times, though, what I really need is a two-hour window of fun—and that means going to the movies!

Full disclosure: I'm a movie fanatic. Going to the movies was a treat when I was growing up, and my parents would take the whole family. When I was in high school, it was a favorite activity with friends. When I was in college at Lawrence University, however, I had no extra money, so going to the movies was a problem. Then I got an idea. I approached the college newspaper and offered to write movie reviews. For four years, I had a free pass to the movies. I saw *every movie released,* which was great fun for me (even if some of the movies weren't very good).

Less successful was taking a date along because I always had to carry a small flashlight so I could take notes during the movie. It was distracting for my date, who was trying to focus on what was happening on the screen, and it hardly made for a romantic evening. To be honest, I wasn't the best reviewer, either. How positive or negative I was about the movie often had more to do about how I felt that day (happy and relaxed or grumpy and tired) than the merits of the film.

All these years later, going to the movies is still my favorite pastime. It's the perfect escape for a couple of hours. Then, when I get back to work, I feel so much better for having taken some time off for stress-releasing fun that I'm twice as productive.

Whether you see a movie, go for a run, or simply sit outside in the fresh air, find what helps you unplug long enough to clear your mind and recharge your batteries. That hour or two is not procrastination. Rather, it's injecting some fun into your life as a way to reduce stress, raise your energy level, and improve your focus.

Rewarding Fun: The Best Incentive

With five children, I can tell you that the promise of fun is a power-ful incentive. When my children were younger, the scenario often went something like this: one (or more) of the children would have a big project or a term paper due the next week. Instead of getting started right away (being planful), they sometimes complained and procrastinated. When they groaned about having to do all that work and thought that it was better to put it off until the weekend, I'd step in with a reward. If they completed the project or term paper *before* the weekend, we'd go to a Cubs game or another special event.

Suddenly everything changed! I'd hardly see them for the next four or five nights after dinner, as they worked on their projects and term papers until everything was done. The result was always far better than if they had stayed up late Sunday night for one long marathon session—and they were able to enjoy some fun as a reward.

The same incentive works for me as well. When I have a big project that looks like it will consume the weekend, Julie sometimes asks if I can find a way to get it done by Friday night. If so, then we can leave Saturday morning and drive to Lake Geneva, Wisconsin (a lovely resort town on a large lake) for the weekend. The thought of two relaxing days of fun is exactly the incentive I need to concentrate on getting the project done ahead of time.

The carrot, as the saying goes, is much more motivating than the stick. Whether you're rewarding someone else or yourself, don't underestimate the promise of fun to increase productivity and improve results.

Spontaneous Fun: The Gift of the Unexpected

Not that long ago, I was working in my office in downtown Chicago when a friend of mine called me. He and his wife had tickets to see the musical *Mamma Mia!* at a theater in Chicago. His wife, who was returning from a business trip, had just called to say her plane was delayed for several hours. Because there was no way his wife could make the show, my friend asked me if I wanted to go.

Until that moment, my plan had been to catch the next train home, but here was an opportunity to enjoy some spontaneous fun. Being planful, I had focused on my priorities for that day and had accomplished everything I needed to do. When I headed home later that night, I was energized and happy. I had a chance to catch up with my friend and an unexpected opportunity to see a show I really enjoy.

I had a similar experience recently while giving a speech in San Francisco. A friend heard I was coming to town and called to ask if I wanted to go to a Giants game. I had planned to fly back to Chicago right after my speech. After reviewing my schedule and priorities, I saw there was no reason I couldn't go to the game and take the red-eye back to Chicago.

Spontaneous fun is like winning the lottery. You don't have to make the arrangements or worry about the logistics. Instead, someone else provides you with an opportunity to have fun, and all you have to do is say yes. In many ways, that makes it twice as much fun.

Surprise Fun: The Joy of the Giver

With spontaneous fun, the gift lands unexpectedly in your lap, thanks to the generosity and thoughtfulness of someone else. With surprise fun, you're the one making the arrangements and being planful for someone else. Usually it's not spontaneous, like a last-minute invitation to a concert, play, or sporting event. It takes some real planning, and that's half the fun for you—while increasing the experience of fun for the other person.

Several years ago, on my mom's 80th birthday, my siblings and I decided to arrange a surprise for her: all five of us children, our spouses, and 14 grandchildren traveled from various parts of the country to Minnesota to surprise her. It took quite a bit of planning to find the best date for us all to be there, the logistics of traveling and finding places to stay, and arranging the restaurant for the surprise birthday dinner. We had to figure out how to get Mom there without her suspecting anything and keep a secret among 24 people. Definitely not easy!

When Mom walked into the restaurant and saw us all there, the look on her face was priceless. I still get emotional just thinking about that moment, how happy she was, and how thrilled all of us were that we'd brought her that joy. In the years since Mom passed away, my siblings and I often recall that surprise dinner. In retelling the story, we relive the experience, which re-creates the fun and makes that memory even more special.

Part of living a values-based life is to ensure that we're accumulating meaningful experiences and creating lasting memories. These moments may be funny childhood memories or poignant times with family and loved ones. Sometimes, it's a moment when our lives changed forever.

When Julie was in her senior year of college and I was working in Chicago, I drove to see her every other weekend. When winter break came, she went home to her parents' house in St. Paul, Minnesota, and I drove up to see her on the weekend, just before Christmas.

Since she was graduating in about six months, I suggested that Julie think about moving to Chicago to find a job.

Julie looked at me. "I don't think I'd just move to Chicago."

All the way back to Chicago, I contemplated her reply. It was clear to me that Julie Jansen wasn't going to move away from her family and live in Chicago unless she had a real incentive. I also realized that if I wasn't smart about this, I could risk losing her. I had to do something—and that gave me an idea of how to surprise her.

I called Julie the following day to tell her that my brother Steve was going to be in St. Paul the next morning and would like to meet her for breakfast. Julie agreed to meet him at a particular restaurant at eight o'clock. I told her I'd get in touch with Steve to confirm the plan, and I'd see her in two weeks.

I drove all night to make it back to Minnesota in time. I parked a block from Julie's house and waited until I saw her walking toward the restaurant. Slowly, I pulled up next to Julie and called out the window. "Hi, Julie, how are you doing?"

Julie stopped and did a double take. "Steve? Harry? Steve?" (My brother and I look a lot alike.) Realizing it was me, Julie was genuinely surprised (and happy) to see me.

"You were just here," she said. "Why did you come back so soon?"

I got out of the car and stood beside her on the snowy sidewalk. "I needed to talk to you about something," I told her. "Will you marry me?"

Over the past 40 years, not a week has passed that I haven't thought about that moment. Julie and I reminisce about it, sometimes teasing each other. It was a very special shared moment, made all the better because it was a surprise for her.

Leveraged Fun: Shared Experiences Pay Dividends

The interconnected nature of our buckets often means that we can increase—or leverage—the benefits in more than one area. As I describe in chapter 6, when my children were younger, I often looked for ways to increase my family time by taking them with me to certain outings—such as going to a Cubs baseball game or a Chicago Bulls basketball game along with business associates and their children. The same happens with fun activities. An exercise class taken with friends can increase fun while also improving health. The same goes for watching a movie while I'm exercising on an elliptical—it's fun *and* I'm getting exercise.

This really isn't multitasking; it's finding ways to leverage activities for more benefits. In fact, this approach can even turn difficult chores into fun. A friend of mine described the unexpected fun she and her siblings had while cleaning out their family home after their parents died. The work was hard and dusty, and more than a little emotional. Taking the time to laugh and share memories, though, actually made it fun.

This is one of those moments when you can take care of more than one life bucket at a time—provided that you're really present and not just putting in an appearance.

Enriching Fun: Engaging Your Mind

Rounding out our list is another kind of fun: the kind that enriches and even teaches while also providing enjoyment. If you're a book lover, you know what I'm talking about. The thought of spending a few hours with your favorite author, a good plot, and engaging characters is fun and enriching. The same goes for seeing a museum exhibit, attending a play, or engaging in another cultural activity. These types of experiences can lift us out of our daily routines and expand our perceptions.

When shared with others, these experiences also generate dividends, just like leveraged fun. Going to a play or a movie with a friend and talking about it afterward can increase enjoyment for both of you and lead to deeper insights. The combination of fun and intellectual stimulation is one reason why people enjoy book clubs: it's social and enriching.

A FULL FUN AGENDA

As you review the seven types of fun, you might wonder which are the best ways to increase your fun bucket. My suggestion is to engage in all of them. Being planful, especially with vacation time, can ensure that you are making fun a priority. Be open to more opportunities to engage in fun—whether it's a reward, a stress relief, something spontaneous, a surprise for someone else, a way to leverage the benefits across multiple buckets, or an enriching activity.

These moments of fun can increase your sense of joy. No matter how busy you are or pressured you feel in other areas of your life, an hour or so of fun can raise your level of happiness and contentment.

Don't wait until some day in the future when you supposedly will have more time, money, or freedom to spend on fun. If that's your approach, that day may never come because you won't know how to unplug and relax. Worse yet, the accumulated stress and pressure can affect your health—and even shorten your life.

Take time for joy, happiness, and fun right here, right now. Your values-based life depends on it.

NEXT STEPS TO BETTER BALANCE

Review the seven components of fun. Reflect on the last time you experienced fun in each category. (If you can't recall a recent example, that tells you something!)

- Planned fun
- Stress-releasing fun
- Rewarding fun
- Spontaneous fun
- Surprise fun
- Leveraged fun
- Enriching fun

As you pursue life balance, what can you do to experience more fun and joy in each of these areas?

CHAPTER 10

FAITH AND SPIRITUALITY: STRENGTH AT THE CORE

My faith is very important to me, to the point that I have a specific bucket to allocate time for prayer and spiritual practice each week. In discussing this, though, it's not my intention to preach or try to convince someone to see things my way. Whether you have a bucket for faith and spirituality is up to you—just like it's your choice as to how to define each of your life buckets. I'm writing this chapter the same way I approach faith and spirituality in my classes on values-based leadership at Kellogg: I share my personal experiences while being sensitive and respectful to the faith traditions, spiritual practices, and perspectives of others.

By being open about my faith and spirituality, I can make it safe and welcoming for others to express and explore their own. No matter how different our perspectives and practices—even when I'm talking with someone who is an agnostic or atheist—as we frame our discussion around living a values-based life, there is much common ground.

Here's how it usually happens in my leadership classes: in the first session of every quarter, I introduce the importance of self-reflection and being self-aware, just as I did in the first chapter of this book. I encourage students to practice turning off the noise and engaging in 15 minutes of reflection daily. I am happy to leave it at that. Then someone usually asks, "How do you do that?" and the conversation goes a little deeper into my daily self-examination of living my values and what I think is most important to me.

Later that evening, I start to get emails from people wanting to take the discussion deeper into spirituality. Some will share that they practiced a faith tradition when they were younger but stopped when they were in high school. Now they're wondering if it's time to reexamine that part of their lives, and they'd like to talk about it. Others don't practice a religion, but they consider themselves to be somewhat spiritual, and they want to talk about taking self-reflection to the next level.

And there are those who would not consider themselves spiritual at all. Yet in talking with them, I can tell they are intrigued by how important it is to me. The question they ask is something like this: "To be an effective leader, do you think it's important to have a spiritual foundation? Is it really necessary?" My answer is straightforward: "I don't know if it is important for other people, but I know I could not be an effective leader without a spiritual foundation." That's the message I'm sharing here, too. This is what works for me and my pursuit of a values-based life.

MY FAITH JOURNEY

Since childhood, I have had a deep sense of faith and spirituality. Some of my earliest memories, going all the way back to when I was about three years old, are of attending church with my family. In those days, the Catholic mass was still said in Latin, which of course I couldn't understand. Yet there was something very special about sitting in that big church, surrounded by hundreds of people who were singing hymns, saying prayers, or sitting quietly and listening to the priest. I understood at a young age that this experience was important to all these people around me, especially my mother and father—and so it became important to me.

As I grew up, my sense of faith deepened, as did my understanding. My parents, who never missed a Sunday service, and my uncle Father Francis (whom I mention in chapter 1) showed me what it meant to live a faith-based life. They gave my siblings and me structure and discipline; missing church just because someone didn't feel like going wasn't an option for us when we were growing up. We went because our parents felt it was important for keeping our faith tradition alive.

Faith, of course, is much more than getting your ticket punched by attending a service or going through the motions. It is a state of mind and a way of behaving in the world—at school, at work, within your family, among friends and acquaintances, and as you interact with people you don't even know. For me, faith in action and values in action stem from the same source: my core religious beliefs and what they teach me about how I should treat others.

THE FAITH BUCKET

The time I devote to my faith includes going to church services, reading scripture, praying regularly (at least once a day), and attending an annual three-day silent retreat. My daily practice of self-reflection, as I described in chapter 1, is tied directly to my religious faith. As I contemplate my values, my sense of purpose, and my priorities of what matters most in my life, I continuously step back and consider the bigger picture. I think about how short life really is—I'm here only for the blink of an eye—which gives me an invaluable perspective. What I do and how I act cannot be about me. Far more important than any success I might achieve is significance, which comes from making a positive difference in the world and being a force for good.

At the end of my life, I want to know that what I did while I was on this earth mattered. This has profound spiritual implications for me. Every day, I strive to use the gifts God has given me to make things better for others. Personally, I believe it's what we're all called to do.

I have no problem talking about any of this with anyone—students, executives, colleagues, or friends—because I believe it's important that we encourage each other to consider the religious or spiritual aspect of our lives. Although I understand that some people prefer to keep a separation between their faith and the rest of their life—and especially their career—that's impossible for me. I cannot separate my faith from my life any more than I can separate my family from my life. The reason is simple: my Christian faith is the foundation of who I am.

FORMING MY IDENTITY

My religious identity formed when I was very young. As I went to Catholic schools, I learned about the teachings of Jesus—about loving God and about loving your neighbor as yourself. My understanding grew with new experiences. For example, when I was an altar boy and served at funeral masses, I was amazed when the priest told grieving people who had lost a loved one that death was also a time for celebration. Their loved one wasn't gone forever; he or she was united with God. The joy came from thinking how this beloved person had gone on ahead to where, one day, we would all be together.

Listening to those words, I began to grasp that this earthly life, although important, wasn't all there was. One day I, too, would no longer be here. What came next in my belief system was heaven and unity with God and all the souls who had gone before us. That was the ultimate goal I set for my life at a young age.

By the time I was in my teenage years, my talks with my uncle Father Francis helped me understand that even though I didn't have a religious calling, I could live my faith in other ways. I committed to setting a positive example through high school and college. I wasn't trying to prove something; I simply thought it was important and consistent with my values. Every Sunday morning during college, I attended mass on campus where I was one of a dozen people. One day, I recognized a young woman who was also a regular. She was a freshman I had seen in the library the first week: Julie Jansen—and by now you know the rest of that story. For 40 years, our shared faith and values have formed a deep bond.

Every aspect of my life has been enhanced by my faith. Julie and I decided, even before we got married, how we would raise our children one day with faith as the foundation. We are fortunate that our five children have embraced their faith. They also support each other when someone gets off track and does or says something that's inconsistent with our values. When our children were all living at home, we attended church as a family. Now that they are older and the eldest children are living on their own, Julie and I remind them that if they say faith is important to them, then surely they can spare a few hours out of their 168 each week to express it.

Over the years, my faith has been a source of strength during times of difficulty. No matter how challenging things are, self-reflection and prayer help me stay centered in doing the right thing and doing the best I can, as I described in chapter 1. At times, I use these words almost like a mantra; they calm and focus me, and it reduces worry, fear, anxiety, pressure, and stress. That's certainly a benefit to my health.

In addition, my faith encourages me to enjoy life, through all the ups and downs. Every day is a gift, meant to be treasured. In that way, my spirituality also increases my sense of fun. One of the greatest gifts of being human is the capacity to experience and share joy. A good laugh, time together with friends and loved ones, being outdoors in nature, taking a walk at night as the stars are just starting to come out—all of these simple pleasures can be spiritual expressions as well.

Another part of my faith is seeking to make a difference. As we discuss in chapter 11, this helps build a legacy as a force multiplier for good, to touch as many people as possible. This isn't about pushing my faith or spiritual views on anyone. Rather, I try to encourage more people to make a difference in their own way, whether by volunteering at a soup kitchen, working with an organization such as Habitat for Humanity, or doing good in their own neighborhood community.

One of the biggest areas affected by my faith—surprisingly, perhaps—has been my career and, in particular, my leadership. In its simplest form, leadership has nothing to do with titles and organizational charts; rather, it has everything to do with the ability to influence others. Because my faith compels me to respect everyone—seeking first to understand rather than to be understood—it helps me relate to others. The more I can relate to others, the better leader I can be. It must be more than just words; there must be action to back it up. As Andrew Carnegie, the industrialist and philanthropist, observed, "As I grow older, I pay less attention to what men say. I just watch what they do."

In each area of my life, I draw on my faith to guide me in living a values-based life. I don't have it all figured out; I'm a work in progress, like everyone else. However, I've been at this a long time, with a well-defined spiritual practice grounded in self-reflection that began more than 40 years ago.

THE THREE-DAY SILENT RETREAT

Every year, over the past four decades, I have attended a three-day silent retreat at the Demontreville Jesuit Retreat House in Lake Elmo, Minnesota. I go the same time every year: the first weekend of December, from Thursday evening through Sunday evening.

This practice wasn't something I sought out. Believe me, given how much I love to talk, I'd never choose a silent retreat for myself. However, when I was first introduced to the retreat, I found it to be a valuable exercise for shutting out the noise and immersing myself in the quiet so I could contemplate the deep questions and listen for how God is talking to me.

My first experience of the retreat was quite a surprise. I had graduated early from college and moved to Evanston, Illinois, just north of Chicago, and was attending Northwestern University's Kellogg School of Management. Every other weekend, I hitchhiked to Lawrence University in Appleton, Wisconsin, to visit Julie, who was still a freshman. Hitchhiking was easy in those days—usually, I'd get a ride with a truck driver making a run from Chicago to Green Bay. (It goes without saying that I would never allow my children to do what I did, nor do I recommend it to anyone else. Forty years ago, however, I could rationalize that it was a good idea, particularly because I had no money.)

Then one day, while at home in Evanston, I received a phone call from Julie's father, inviting me to visit him in St. Paul, Minnesota. I was a little unsure what this was all about, but the visit was important to Julie, so of course I agreed to go. The airfare was cheap, and I flew to the Twin Cities. It was the first weekend in December, and it felt like 20 degrees below zero when I landed.

Julie's father met me at the airport and told me he'd like the two of us to do something together. My first thought was maybe we'd go to a Minnesota Vikings football game.

"This is something I do every year and I would like you to join me," Mr. Jansen said. "It's a retreat."

When I asked him what a retreat was, he explained that it meant time spent in prayer, reflection, and thinking about your values and your purpose. I also suspected he wanted me to think about my relationship with his daughter.

As I was thinking about all this, Mr. Jansen told me one more thing. "It's a silent retreat. You are not going to talk for the next three days."

Now, I usually have difficulty shutting up for three minutes, so three days seemed completely impossible. I knew I could turn around, take the next flight, and be back in Chicago in 45 minutes. Being a finance guy, though, I was familiar with the concept of sunk cost—money that had already been spent and couldn't be recovered. Because I'd already paid for the trip, I figured I might as well try this retreat thing and see what it was all about.

We drove about ten miles from St. Paul to the Demontreville Jesuit Retreat House in Lake Elmo, Minnesota. There, I was given a name badge and assigned to a room with a single bed, a Bible, and a cup for water. The rules were explained (especially the one about no talking). Every two or three hours, the bell rang, and we gathered in the chapel where one of the Jesuits gave a brief talk meant to help us with our self-reflection and self-examination. Then all 65 men on the retreat headed back to our rooms or took a walk along the lake.

Although the silent part was challenging at first, I understood that if I wanted to communicate with God, I had to "dispose myself"—that was the term Father Ed Sthokal used. In other words, I had to be quiet and listen. As I engaged in self-reflection (asking myself many of the questions that I related in chapter 1), I thought more deeply about things than I ever had before. I cannot say for sure that I heard God talking to me, but I did gain more clarity and perspective in that weekend than I'd ever had in my life.

It was so powerful to be among a group of men attending this retreat. Day or night, there was always someone on the walking paths. Sometimes when I passed a man on the path along the lake, I would notice he looked emotional. A pat on the shoulder or an exchange of nods allowed us to connect without breaking our silence.

On Sunday evening, as we gathered in the cafeteria for a last meal together, the Jesuits announced that we could talk. Quiet conversations began, but no one rushed into animated discussions. Before we departed, one of the Jesuits explained that this retreat should not be a one-time exercise. Rather, it was an introduction to the daily 15-minute exercise of self-reflection. I left that first retreat thinking that I'd try it for a week. After the first week, I thought daily self-examination was valuable to me, so I'd keep it up for another month or two. Now it's been 40 years and counting.

The following December, when Julie's father invited me to attend the retreat again, I met him at the airport in the Twin Cities, and we drove to Lake Elmo. Since then, I've never missed a year—even when I became CFO of Baxter and then chairman and CEO. To completely unplug from the world isn't as hard as you might think. When I arrive at the retreat on Thursday night, I have no phone, no laptop. As the retreat leader reminds us, there is nothing that will happen in the next three days that others can't handle until we return on Monday morning.

Even now, with my schedule of teaching, board meetings, and giving speeches, I'm usually out of the country for at least one week a month. Yet, as the first weekend of December approaches, I know where I will be. I've never changed weekends, even though the Jesuits give 47 weekend retreats at Demontreville every year. As I mentioned in chapter 7, these men with whom I have attended the retreat every year are part of my community. The faces are familiar as we find our regular places in the chapel—I sit in the third row, on the right side, on the aisle. No matter that we don't talk, we still connect.

Whenever I mention the retreat to my students at Kellogg, many of them are very curious about it. They see me as a guy who likes to talk a lot, and often very quickly, yet I find it very valuable to spend three full days in silence. The question I can read on their faces is, "What's that about?" Just the other day I received an email from a student wanting more details about the silent retreat and how to sign up.

Over the years, out of the 70 or so students I teach every quarter, about seven or eight will ask me questions about these retreats. Some have a faith practice but never experienced a retreat before. Some aren't spiritual at all, but now that they're practicing self-reflection, they think the idea of a silent retreat is at least "interesting." Others see me as someone who became CEO of a $10 billion company at age 43. If a silent retreat got me there, then sign them up!

I answer the questions I'm asked. I'm not trying to sell anyone on anything. Teaching at a secular university, I'm well aware of the importance of separating church and state, as they say. At the same time, I've never kept my faith a secret or tried to separate it from any other part of my life. My faith defines me.

FOCUSING ON THE COMMON GROUND

Everybody is different; what works well for one person may not work for another. At the same time, I'm reminded that what unites us is far greater and more powerful than anything that separates us. Many years ago, while I was chairman and CEO of Baxter, I was fortunate to have the opportunity to attend the World Economic Forum in Davos, Switzerland. Beyond the celebrities and the big egos, the experience was amazing because of the collective wisdom. At the forum, deep and important ideas are discussed by bright and insightful minds. Attending the forum was like being back in a liberal arts college.

I recall listening to a phenomenal panel on spirituality and world religions. The panel discussed what was most important in each of the major religions represented: Hindu, Buddhist, Jewish, Muslim, Christian, and other traditions. As I listened, I was struck by the fact that 98 percent of what they discussed were common values, such as treating others with respect and caring for those in need. Unfortunately, in daily life, so much attention is often paid to the small differences that we humans allow to become divisions.

Years later, I invited a group of Kellogg students from multiple faiths—Islam, Judaism, Hinduism, Bahá'í Faith, and Christianity—to an interfaith service at my home. It was a beautiful spring day by Lake Michigan as we gathered in my backyard to share this incredible experience of prayers and readings from each tradition. We acknowledged the richness of our differences and celebrated the unity of what our faiths teach us about love and respect for one another. It reminded me, yet again, of the vast common ground among us.

No matter what we believe or don't believe, most of us find it valuable to ponder the deeper questions: who am I? What is my purpose? What gives my life meaning? We may approach these questions differently. For some, these questions are best contemplated in the context of their faith tradition or spiritual practices. Others may view them in the context of what it means to be human. Whatever path we take, the questions draw us along journeys that are surprisingly similar in many ways.

SHARING STORIES AND EXPERIENCES

A very meaningful experience for me is to have discussions with others about their faith and what it means in their lives. I've had conversations with people from many backgrounds and traditions. What connects us deeply is how our faith tradition has formed our identity. As we share the story of our faith journeys, we are telling each other who we really are.

Jeffrey Solomon, chairman and CEO of Cowen Inc., whose story I shared in chapter 7, told me that in the past few years he has become more comfortable sharing his Jewish faith publicly. The catalyst was Rosh Hashanah in 2017, the Jewish New Year and the first of the High Holy Days ushering in a ten-day period of prayer, reflection, and atonement. Inspired by the beauty of Rosh

Hashanah, Jeff wrote a column to his entire firm about the concept of spiritual rebirth.

When Jeff and I spoke about his thoughts on faith and living a values-based life, it was right before Rosh Hashanah 2019. The timing was perfect for our conversation. "During these ten days, I am more self-reflective. I am taking stock," Jeff said. "Even if you are not Jewish, you can still experience that spiritual rebirth for yourself. It helps you be a better person."

Jeff has shared other reflections from his faith—most profoundly when he wrote a tribute about the Tree of Life Synagogue in Pittsburgh, Pennsylvania, his home faith community. On October 27, 2018, Tree of Life was the setting of unspeakable horror when a gunman committed a mass shooting in which 11 people—including four known to Jeff's family—were killed during Shabbat morning services.

The next day, Jeff wrote a long, emotional message to his entire firm, describing the Tree of Life Synagogue community, where he and his brother, Kyle, spent much of their childhood attending Hebrew school, studying to become a Bar Mitzvah, and learning how to practice the values of *Tzdakah* (charity) and *Tikkun Olam* (repairing the world). He expressed his raw feelings as he began the long process of coming to grips with what had happened: "When pure evil hits your home, everything changes. Suddenly you feel a part of every tragedy that has ever occurred since the dawn of time. You feel a sense of helplessness and deep emptiness. You realize in an instant just how vulnerable we all are to senseless acts of rage and violence."

Since the Tree of Life tragedy, Jeff has been focused on doing more good in the world. "If you know me, you know two things about me: I am Jewish, and I am from Pittsburgh," Jeff told me. "I live the Jewish ideals—among them Tikkun Olam, 'repairing the world,' which I think we all should be doing."

In a note to his firm to mark the one-year anniversary of the Tree of Life mass shooting, Jeff outlined four things he consciously tries to do every day. First on Jeff's list is to remove the "four-letter 'H-Word' from my vocabulary." In reflecting on this, I thought of how casually we throw around the word *hate*—whether we're describing some annoyance or displeasure or we're very angry at someone or something. Banishing the word *hate* from our collective vocabulary is an important first step toward eradicating it from our actions.

His second item is to "consciously try to make two or three people smile every day." Jeff's pursuit resonates with me. A core tenet of both a values-based life and living one's faith is to respect and honor each person. This can be expressed in the simplest ways, such as saying hello, asking someone about his or her family, or exchanging a comment that makes someone smile. To me, that says, "I see you—you matter to me." Everyone is deserving of respect.

Third on Jeff's list is a recommitment to "consciously do One Good Deed a Day." While he has kept true to that task over the past few years, now he mentally links those acts to the friends who were lost at Tree of Life. "Because they were all such good people, it's my own personal way of staying connected to their lives. And I am grateful to know I am perpetuating their own good nature in my daily routine," Jeff wrote.

I reflected on Jeff's words and how they set an example for all of us. In doing good on behalf of and in memory of others, we spread love and positivity in the world.

Last but certainly not least on Jeff's list, he shares that he has become more open about his Judaism. "Not that I ever denied it, but it's not like I really ever talked about it specifically. It's also not like I talk about it all the time." Given his connection with Tree of Life and the fact that people know he is Jewish, Jeff has embraced these opportunities to talk about his faith and religion in general. "This has fostered more dialogue about the religious views and beliefs of others than I have ever had, which in turn has actually helped me understand that most religions have way more in common than not. It has also given me hope that open-minded practitioners of faiths other than my own as well as open-minded people who choose not to follow a religion can actually find commonality if they want to do so, even as we respect our differences."

To that profound sentiment, I can only add a most sincere "Amen." Although religion, sadly, has been a source of division in this world for centuries, it is *people* who have taken up those destructive causes. As we embrace what it means to be a person of faith in any creed or context, we can see that there is so much more that unites us.

Much of that common ground is found in selflessness, in putting others before ourselves. As C. S. Lewis wrote in *Mere Christianity*, "The principle runs through all life from top to bottom. Give up yourself, and you will find your real self. Lose your life and you will save it . . . ."[1]

In its essence, spiritual practice of any kind is never about any of us—rather, it's about all of us. Although our rituals and traditions are meaningful to us, we cannot allow our personal religious identities to become false divisions that separate us from those who believe or think differently. Rather, we all share profound truths of love, compassion, and forgiveness. No one owns any of them. With respect and understanding of others' practices, we are able to see these truths through multiple lenses. Then we're not limited by our own myopia; we see more clearly and broadly.

Khalid Ali, a close friend and former Kellogg student, draws on his Islamic faith to guide his life. "I grew up on a farm in western Pennsylvania in a very religious household," Khalid shared. "In between cleaning out the sheep manure from the barn, milking the goats, and feeding the chickens, I prayed five times a day, attended Friday prayers, and memorized much of the Quran. Also, I never drank alcohol or ate pork." As he got older and started college, Khalid found himself questioning some tenets of his faith and grappling with what it means to be a Muslim living in America. "9/11 pushed Islam and Muslims into the spotlight in a very negative way, but the reality is that it had been difficult to be 'publicly Muslim' in America for long before then—certainly for as long as I can remember," Khalid told me. Yet he never abandoned his faith.

"In college I was elected class president all four years, and despite attending nearly every social gathering, I never once drank alcohol. Through Islam I had a grounding that continued to guide my moral compass and self-discipline. Fundamentally, Islam gave me the tools and a language to commune with a Higher Being and appreciate the magnanimity of that Being and the beauty that exists all around us," Khalid said.

In our class at Kellogg on values-based leadership and discussions about self-reflection, Khalid said he began to reexamine the values and faith foundation of his youth in the context of values-based leadership. "Most probably due to my religious upbringing, I felt an immediate connection to the concept of a values-based approach to life," he said.

Now living in Philadelphia with his wife and two children, Khalid makes a concerted effort to foster understanding and cohesion among his neighbors. "Neighborhood and community are very important in Islam," Khalid said. Rather than try to hide their religion, Khalid and his wife, Leena, have made a conscious decision to share their traditions with their neighbors. For example, during the month of Ramadan, when Muslims all over the world fast from dawn to sunset for 30 days, Khalid, Leena, and the children share platters of traditional *iftaar* food (the meal with which Muslims break their daily fast) with their majority non-Muslim neighbors, along with a brief written explanation of their observance. During Christmas, which Khalid's family does not celebrate, Leena bakes cookies and other sweets as a gift to neighbors, along with a card explaining how Jesus is revered as a prophet in the Islamic faith, and his mother, Mary (or Miriam), is the only woman mentioned directly by name in the Quran.

"To me, good food is one of the best ways to bring people together—and Leena is a wonderful chef," Khalid said. "We have received an outpouring of positive responses from our neighbors, thanking us for sharing our faith and our culture."

Through their willingness to be open and transparent, Khalid and his family consciously build bridges with their neighbors and, by extension, a broader community. "America is described as a melting pot, but we like to think of it as a 'potluck'—everybody has something to bring to the table," Khalid said. "As we come together from different faiths and share what we believe, we have the opportunity to experience new perspectives and learn from each other."

WHEREVER YOU ARE, START THERE

If you think it's important to have a bucket for faith or spirituality, it is up to you to decide what types of activities and commitments are important. You may be part of a faith community and regularly attend services. Or you may consider yourself to be spiritual without any defined religious practice. It may be that you feel disconnected from the faith tradition of your childhood, or perhaps you were not raised with a faith tradition. Now you may be open to exploring new traditions and ways of expressing a connection to something greater than yourself. For some, spending time in nature or contemplating deep, existential questions may be meaningful as a way to transcend daily experience. One spiritual practice that many people find meaningful is mindfulness, which is a type of meditation in which you intently focus on what you're seeing, hearing, sensing, and feeling in the moment.

Wherever you are, start there. Whether it's meditation, prayer, or religious practice, find what nourishes you and gives you a sense of being connected to something larger than yourself. It may involve returning to your spiritual roots and practicing the faith you knew as a child. Or you may be on a journey—a spiritual quest—to find what speaks to you.

For me, the journey always takes me deeper into the roots of my faith. The beliefs and practices remind me of who I am, where I belong, and where I hope to be at the end of my life.

NEXT STEPS TO BETTER BALANCE

As you contemplate all aspects of what it means to live a values-based life, consider what part spiritual or religious practices might play for you.

- **Do you consider yourself religious or spiritual? Are you both—or neither?** If it's been some time since you've contemplated these questions, the answers may require some reflection.
- **Did you grow up in a faith tradition? How is it meaningful to you now?** Have you been positively influenced by the faith of your childhood to hold certain values or act a certain way today?
- **How, where, and when do you contemplate the big questions of life?** At one time or another, all of us have wondered about why we're here, what the purpose of our life is, what meaning there is in this life. Do you explore that in meditation, in prayer, or in other ways, such as being in nature?
- **Is there any particular faith, tradition, or practice that appeals to you?** If you feel a tug in a particular direction, what's stopping you from exploring what it might mean for you?

For me, nothing captures the spiritual core of a values-based life more than "The Peace Prayer" attributed to St. Francis of Assisi (and shared on the website of the National Shrine of St. Francis of

Assisi).[2] Regardless of your belief system, tradition, or philosophy, consider these words:

> Lord, make me an instrument of Thy peace;
> Where there is hatred, let me sow love;
> Where there is injury, pardon;
> Where there is error, the truth;
> Where there is doubt, the faith;
> Where there is despair, hope;
> Where there is darkness, light;
> And where there is sadness, joy.

* * *

> O Divine Master,
> Grant that I may not so much seek
> To be consoled, as to console;
> To be understood, as to understand;
> To be loved as to love.

* * *

> For it is in giving that we receive;
> It is in pardoning that we are pardoned;
> And it is in dying that we are born to eternal life. Amen.

CHAPTER 11

MAKING A DIFFERENCE: THE LEGACY YOU LEAVE

Now we come to the last life bucket, which by no means is the least. In fact, this bucket has an impact that goes well beyond your own life and your immediate circle of family and friends. This bucket is how, in big and small ways, you can help change the world.

For some people, making a difference is a strong motivation in their lives. Perhaps service to others is important in their families, and they have been volunteering in the community and for charity projects since they were young. This is certainly true of many purpose-driven millennials today. When I was a student at Kellogg many years ago, no more than 5 percent of my classmates were involved with nonprofit organizations or charitable work in any way. Today it's the opposite. More than 90 percent of current Kellogg students are active in nonprofits and philanthropy. Some volunteer with charities and service organizations—among them is Kellogg Cares, which focuses on meaningful service opportunities in the local community. Other Kellogg students are pursuing a career in the nonprofit sector and are highly motivated to put their MBA degrees to work in addressing major societal issues.

Other people, though, are not involved in volunteering, charitable work, or socially responsible activities. No shame or judgment here—just an invitation to think about what each of us can do.

I've found that the desire to make a difference is one of those wake-up calls that many of us experience at some point in our lives. It can happen after you realize just how fast the last 10 or 20 years went by. It seemed like yesterday when you were in college. Or perhaps you have attended the funeral of someone close to your age—a friend you knew in high school or college. Suddenly, you're thinking about how short life really is. As you engage in self-reflection, you ask yourself, "What difference am I making while I am here, on this planet?"

You may attend a memorial service for someone who lived a long and meaningful life—perhaps a relative or someone else close to you. You listen to the eulogy and the many stories told about all the good this person did to touch people's lives. Afterward, you ask yourself, "What will others say about me when I'm gone? Am I making a difference at all? How am I helping others, especially those who are less fortunate?"

These are sobering questions. Instead of viewing them as punitive or scolding, however, allow them to be enlightening and inspiring. Pondering these questions can lead you to discover how you can, in your own way, help make the world a better place.

NOT BEING POSSESSED BY POSSESSIONS

Taking care of others who are less fortunate is a lesson I learned early in life. When I was a youngster in Catholic schools, we collected money for the poor during Lent. Some of those dimes and quarters came from our allowances, which gave us an early taste of what it was like to make a sacrifice for the sake of others. It was a formative experience. I learned that even though I didn't have everything I wanted (like that new baseball glove I had my eye on), I still had more than many other people. With this perspective, I stopped focusing on what I didn't have and what I wanted and began to consider the needs of others.

I wasn't just being selfless. As I collected more money, I started to feel really good about it. Suddenly, I saw that collecting and donating all those dimes and quarters made me feel happier than I would have been with a new baseball glove.

My dad worked hard to provide for our family, but he never made it all about money. As I relate in chapter 1, he used to say, "Have you ever seen a hearse going to a cemetery with a U-Haul attached to it?" Every time I heard him say that line, I knew that it was important to keep material possessions in perspective.

When I was in college, one of my roommates had much the same attitude. Brian always bought his clothes at Goodwill, not because he couldn't afford anything new, but because he just didn't see the need for it. I can remember walking through downtown Appleton, Wisconsin, where Lawrence University is located, and asking Brian about a secondhand raincoat he was wearing.

To explain his preference for shopping at Goodwill, Brian told me about his aunt whose prized possession was a new mink stole. "When she goes to a restaurant, she can't check it for fear someone will steal it. She's so worried about her fur, she won't even leave it on the back of the chair when she goes to the restroom. Instead, she brings it with her."

Then, to my shock, Brian pulled off his old raincoat, threw it in a puddle, and stomped on it. "I don't ever want to worry about material things. It's not worth it!" As Brian picked up his wet coat and put it back on, his message was clear. He was never going to be possessed by his possessions.

When Julie and I got married, we didn't have much money, so we were never really motivated by material things. As our careers advanced, we made sure our lifestyle didn't change very much.

We never wanted to become overly focused on things that didn't really matter. For example, when I was named CEO of Baxter, it really was a proud moment. I had more responsibilities and I reported directly to the company's board of directors. Other than that, things didn't change all that much in my life. I still drove my six-year-old Toyota to work, and my family lived in the same house we owned since I was a senior analyst.

No matter how much money we made, Julie and I were determined that things would not change because, believe me, when you reach a certain point in your career, there are plenty of temptations that can make you forget who you are. Focusing on the needs of others can help prevent that from happening.

DO YOU HAVE ENOUGH TO SHARE?

Let's assume that you are motivated to make a difference. The problem, though, is that as you think about all the issues in the world—poverty, hunger, illiteracy, debilitating diseases, the digital divide, and the environment, just to name a few—it feels overwhelming. You're just one person. How can you solve problems that are truly global in scale? Given your salary and free time, you can't even make the slightest dent. It's easy to let such thinking overwhelm you.

Perhaps you are in the first years of your career and getting ahead consumes a great deal of your time and attention. Along with that, you may be in a long-term relationship or married; perhaps you have children or are planning to have a family. As you think about these obligations and how much time, energy, and money they require, you just don't see that there is much left over to help others. Maybe you are further along in your career, but you're saving for retirement, sending your children to college, or have other family obligations such as caring for aging parents. As you see it, you just don't have much extra to give to charity or help solve the problems of the world.

Whatever your life scenario, it's easy to convince yourself that you should wait until later when you (supposedly) will have more time and money. The only problem is, if helping others isn't a priority now, how can you be sure that you will suddenly focus on it when you're making more money and living a more comfortable lifestyle? Doing good is a habit, just like exercise and engaging in a spiritual practice.

Another thing to consider is what you have to share—it could be more than you realize, based on the amount of money you need to lead a satisfying life. Although this is highly personal and also depends on where you live and the cost of living, there is evidence that a higher income does not lead to greater happiness and well-being. In an article in *Nature Human Behaviour,* researchers Andrew Jebb, Louis Tay, Ed Diener, and Shigehiro Oishi explained their findings using Gallup World Poll data from more than 1.7 million people worldwide. The goal was to identify what they called "income satiation"—or the point at which a higher income did not make a difference to the person's life. For emotional well-being, that satiation point was between \$60,000 and \$75,000 a year.[1]

I'm certainly not suggesting that you should cap your earnings or slow down your career. Instead, think about what money really means in your life. After you've taken care of your basic needs and a few comforts, you may find that the pursuit of more money actually diminishes your life satisfaction. As the alternative to getting on that hamster wheel of chasing more and more possessions, consider what is enough—and how much you can share with others.

YOU ARE "THOSE GUYS"

If you want to live in a better world, you can't simply wait for someone else to step in and do the hard work. Early in my career, I observed a common assumption and widespread expectation that all the problems would be solved by a group of people known as "those guys"—a gender-neutral term referring to people in charge. In the workplace, many people working in cubicles and on the front lines thought they couldn't possibly change things or have an impact. As it turned out, their assumptions were wrong.

As I realized then, and as I tell people today, each of us has the ability to be one of those guys. We can exert a positive influence, starting with our own behavior, the example we set, and our interactions with others. Although it's true that the rich and powerful have much more money and influence to put to work for the benefit of others, we can do the same. If each of us believes strongly in bringing about positive change in the world, we cannot leave it to someone else.

In other words, you are those guys! Rather than waiting for someone else to show up, be willing to look at what you can do. It can be as simple as being a good person and showing gratitude and appreciation for others. Living the Golden Rule—treating others the way you want to be treated—means showing respect to everyone you meet. Now imagine the force multiplier if everyone committed to doing the same thing.

Look for ways to make a difference. No positive action is too small—even if it's just smiling at people and saying hello. If you doubt the impact of doing that, just consider the last time someone greeted you warmly and how that made you feel. There is no shortage of good works you can do in your neighborhood (shoveling the walk for your elderly neighbors) or in your community (participating in food drives or picking up litter in the park). On a global level, you can join with millions of other people who want to make a difference, either by making a donation, spreading awareness of the problem, or getting directly involved.

Don't wait until some undefined point in the future when you will have more money, time, and connections. Instead, think about your legacy as a journey. Along the way, you prepare and practice, just like you would do for playing a sport or running a marathon.

The small steps you take today will give you a foundation on which to build a legacy of doing good for others and making a positive impact.

PAYING BACK BY PAYING IT FORWARD

Another motivation for making a difference is paying back the kindnesses and assistance we've received in our lives. Khalid Ali, my good friend and former student whose story I shared in chapter 10, told me recently that he often reflects on how others encouraged and helped him when he was younger. "I feel so incredibly lucky that throughout my life there were people—not just relatives and friends but also complete strangers who I may not have had anything in common with except our shared humanity—who were willing to go out of their way to give me opportunities, such as scholarships for college," Khalid said. "I am deeply indebted to them for helping me achieve my personal and professional aspirations."

To show his gratitude for what he received, Khalid said he makes an effort to "pay forward what I can never pay back." This includes helping his community, volunteering, and showing kindness and understanding to others. By sharing these experiences whenever possible with their children, Khalid and his wife, Leena, strive to set a positive example. "Of course, we've had bad experiences with people, too, but for us, it boils down to focusing on and nurturing the good in ourselves and others," Khalid said.

In the same way, with everything you do to make a positive difference, you are setting an example for others. If you have children, even small acts of charity and kindness can convey your family values. There are many ways to become involved in your local community, from a one-time event to ongoing volunteering. Your faith community may also be involved in community projects, such as soup kitchens, food pantries, or programs for underprivileged youth. As you get involved, you can encourage others to do the same. Suddenly, the efforts of one person can grow fivefold, tenfold, and even more!

SAVING THE WORLD

As you reflect on what you might do, never underestimate a genuine desire to make a difference. The most inspiring example I know is Andrew Youn, a 2006 graduate of Kellogg, who could have easily pursued a career in the for-profit world. Instead, Andrew pursued his passion for helping farm families in Sub-Saharan Africa, especially the children at risk of dying from hunger-related causes. In his second year at Kellogg, Andrew began pursuing a business solution. In March 2006, he cofounded One Acre Fund as a nonprofit social enterprise that provides smallholder farmers with seed, fertilizer, training, and better access to the marketplace. Today, One Acre Fund serves more than 1 million farm families in Kenya, Rwanda, Uganda, Tanzania, Burundi, and Malawi. (To read more about the amazing work of One Acre Fund, please visit www.OneAcreFund.org.) In honor of his work and example, Andrew received an honorary Doctor of Humane Letters degree from Northwestern University and was the commencement speaker at Kellogg's 2019 MBA convocation.

Among the many amazing things about Andrew's story is that he did not come from an agricultural background. He had no long-term ties with Africa when he dreamed of starting One Acre Fund. Rather, he saw a problem and realized he could apply his Kellogg MBA and his network to make an enormous difference. Andrew has provided many of us with the pleasure of helping support this mission. Although most of us will never do what he did—move to Africa (he currently lives full-time in Rwanda with his family) and devote himself to solving a problem on a global scale—we can be a small part of it. Many Kellogg students, both Andrew's former classmates and others in subsequent classes who have heard about his work, support One Acre Fund with donations. I, too, am proud to be a One Acre Fund supporter, including by donating all proceeds from the sales of my three books and all my speaking fees to One Acre Fund.

It wasn't enough for me to just send money, however; I wanted to see the work of One Acre Fund in action and to share the experience with my wife and children. In 2016, we traveled to Kenya to visit farms where One Acre Fund is bringing help and hope. We saw firsthand that One Acre Fund's work is not a handout; rather, it's providing empowerment through training and low-cost loans to help farmers grow their way out of poverty. And it all started with one person who wanted to make a difference.

WHERE YOUR PASSIONS LIE

What difference will you make? Perhaps your talent, experience, and passion will lead you to explore becoming involved in a particular mission or to tackle a specific problem. You may follow the path Andrew did and devote 100 percent of your time and talent to this mission. Or you may be like many of us who find ways to get involved through volunteering and making donations.

There is no shortage of places or opportunities to get involved in doing good works. With self-reflection, you will likely see more ways in which you can make a difference. Some of these opportunities may even come to you.

When I left Baxter and began considering what I would do in the next phase of my life, I was approached by Dean Donald Jacobs of Kellogg about teaching. My first response was that I didn't have a PhD, so how could I become a university professor? Dean Jacobs assured me that I could be a clinical professor and share my corporate career with students. As I reflected on the opportunity, and given the fact I had been a CFO, I realized that I could possibly teach finance classes. However, I felt a calling in a different direction. I wanted to apply the experiences and lessons learned from every aspect of my life. Dean Jacobs encouraged me, and I have taught values-based leadership for the past 15 years.

Teaching values-based leadership has brought numerous benefits: helping shape the next generation of leaders at Kellogg with values-based leadership, writing books and giving speeches about values-based leadership to organizations around the world, and donating all my book sales and speech proceeds to One Acre Fund. As I told Dean Jacobs a few years ago, "It's a trifecta!"

Dean Jacobs smiled at me and shook his head. "No, Harry, it's not a trifecta—it's a 'four-fecta' because you also love doing it."

Since Dean Jacobs's death in 2017 at the age of 90, I have often reflected on his words and how they inspire me to continue my efforts to make a difference anywhere I can. Although I am doing my best to help others, I also receive the benefits of joy and satisfaction.

THE GOOD THAT YOU DO

If you believe that you should devote some of your 168 to making a difference and leaving a legacy, open your mind and your heart to the possibilities. No matter where you are in life, you can give of yourself—time, talent, and treasure. Don't wait to make a difference, because right now the world needs what you can give, whether that's a donation to a good cause or a smile to someone who could really use some cheering up.

Yes, you can and should enjoy a good life and the fruits of your labors. By committing a portion of your 168 to doing good in the world, you also can make a positive impact far beyond what you thought possible. Not only will you help improve the lives of other people but also they, in turn, may be inspired to help someone else. In addition, as the people around you observe what you are doing, they may decide to help as well. By giving of yourself, you can make an investment that pays big dividends. Your values-based life will truly make a difference—for yourself, your loved ones, and the world.

NEXT STEPS TO BETTER BALANCE

Although there is no shortage of opportunities to do good in the world, you probably have more passion or interest in specific areas. Here are some questions to help you discover where you can make a difference in the world. The sooner you start, the better for all involved.

- What issues in the world, causes, or problems ignite your passion and desire to help others?
- What talents or experiences make you uniquely qualified to address specific areas?
- Do you have a personal or family connection to a cause?
- Are your friends or colleagues involved in a charity or other activity that you would like to support with your time, talent, or treasure?

EPILOGUE: YOUR VALUES-BASED LIFE JOURNEY CONTINUES

With your life buckets in place and your time allocated according to your values and priorities, you are about to embark on a journey. You're aware by now that the destination of being in balance all the time can never be reached. What matters most is the effort you make to pursue a values-based life.

Living a values-based life starts with what I call the four principles of values-based leadership (as I outlined in the introduction). In the context of your 168, think of them as the four principles of a values-based life.

The first and most important principle is self-reflection, which goes right back to our discussion in chapter 1. You need to know your values, what matters most to you, what you believe in, and what you stand for. Self-reflection helps you keep your commitments to yourself and others, and increases your awareness of how you treat people and whether the way you act is aligned with your values.

The second principle is balance and perspective, which emphasizes the importance of understanding diverse viewpoints and opinions. In a world that's more divided than ever, you need balance and perspective to foster empathy and encourage meaningful discussions. This thinking can reduce conflict while embracing and celebrating our differences.

The third principle of true self-confidence enables you to know your strengths and acknowledge your weaknesses. If you're motivated to become part of the force for good by volunteering or engaging in other positive actions, true self-confidence can empower you to channel your abilities and interests.

The fourth principle of genuine humility reminds you of the importance of showing respect to all people, regardless of who they are, where they come from, and how alike or different they are from you. Genuine humility encourages you to make an extra effort to welcome others, particularly those who are fearful or vulnerable.

These four principles are the backbone of living a values-based life. Not only will these principles enrich your satisfaction but also they will enable you to become a role model within your family, among your friends and acquaintances, and as you interact with others—making the most of your 168.

Each week, you only have 168 hours—no more or less; it's up to you to decide how to allocate them. I know from 40 years of personal experience that self-reflection is the best way to pursue a values-based life. There is no pattern or prescription that will fit everyone; you must make your life bucket choices based on what matters most to you—right now, in your current circumstances.

If you want to live a life with more purpose, meaning, engagement, satisfaction, and fun, you can begin the journey today. It takes effort, but the pursuit of a values-based life is its own reward.

NOTES

CHAPTER 1

1. Tasha Eurich, "What Self-Awareness Really Is (and How to Cultivate It)," *Harvard Business Review,* January 4, 2018.

CHAPTER 2

1. David Whitford, "The Strange Existence of Ram Charan," *Fortune,* April 24, 2007.
2. Barbranda Lumpkins Walls, "Haven't Done a Will Yet?" AARP .org, February 24, 2017.

CHAPTER 3

1. Markus Christen and Ruskin M. Morgan, "Keeping Up with the Joneses: Analyzing the Effect of Income Inequality on Consumer Borrowing," *Quantitative Marketing and Economics,* June 2005.

CHAPTER 4

1. Charles Duhigg, *The Power of Habit: Why We Do What We Do in Life and Business* (New York: Random House, 2012), p. 63.
2. Ibid., p. 51.

CHAPTER 6

1. Chip Cutter, "When These Executives Want Candid Advice, They Text," *The Wall Street Journal,* October 14, 2019.
2. Sylvia Ann Hewlett, "Executive Women and the Myth of Having It All," *Harvard Business Review,* April 2002.

CHAPTER 7

1. Oprah Winfrey, "Oprah Opens Up about How She Defines the Word 'Family,'" *O, The Oprah Magazine,* February 6, 2019.
2. David W. McMillan and David M. Chavis, "Sense of Community: A Definition and Theory," *Journal of Community Psychology,* January 1986.
3. Annie McKee, "Happiness Traps," *Harvard Business Review,* September–October 2017.

CHAPTER 8

1. Jim Loehr and Tony Schwartz, "The Making of a Corporate Athlete," *Harvard Business Review,* January 2001.
2. Christopher M. Barnes, "Sleep Well, Lead Better," *Harvard Business Review,* September–October 2018.
3. Ruth Umoh, "Arianna Huffington Says She Became Successful after She Quit One Common Bad Habit," CNBC.com, March 11, 2018.
4. Barnes, "Sleep Well, Lead Better."
5. National Sleep Foundation, "The Complex Relationship between Sleep, Depression & Anxiety," 2019, https://www.sleepfoundation.org/articles/complex-relationship-between-sleep-depression-anxiety.
6. National Institute of Mental Health, "Statistics," 2019, https://www.nimh.nih.gov/health/statistics/index.shtml.

7. Loehr and Schwartz, "The Making of a Corporate Athlete."
8. Ibid.

CHAPTER 9

1. Mayo Clinic, "Stress Management," April 5, 2019, https://www.mayoclinic.org/healthy-lifestyle/stress-management/in-depth/stress-relief/art-20044456.
2. Brené Brown, "The Very Best Resolution You Can Make This Year," *O, The Oprah Magazine,* January 2014.
3. Amy Hinote, *The Power of a Vacation: 365 Quotes, Verses, and Facts That Remind Us of the Importance of Taking a Vacation* (Fairhope, AL: VRM Intel Magazine, 2017).

CHAPTER 10

1. C. S. Lewis, *Mere Christianity* (New York: Macmillan Publishing Company, 1943, 1945, 1952).
2. National Shrine of Saint Francis of Assisi, "The Peace Prayer," http://www.shrinesf.org/franciscan-prayer.html.

CHAPTER 11

1. Andrew Jebb, Louis Tay, Ed Diener, and Shigehiro Oishi, "Happiness, Income Satiation, and Turning Points around the World," *Nature Human Behaviour,* January 2018.

INDEX

Page references followed by *fig* indicate an illustrated figure; followed by *t* indicate a table.